THE MIRACLE FLIGHT
OF JULIANE KOEPCKE

In 1971, a delicate seventeen-year-old girl named Juliane Koepcke was flying from her home in Lima, Peru, to a remote town in the Peruvian jungle. She was sitting in a window seat in the rear of the plane when the pilot asked the passengers to fasten their seatbelts. Suddenly the airliner was engulfed in a violent jungle storm, and Juliane saw a brilliant flash. Flames tore over the right wing, and the plane began to disintegrate in mid-flight.

Juliane felt herself twisting and whirling as she fell through the air, and then blacked out. The next thing she remembered was the sound of jungle birds around her: she found herself lying on the shaded floor of the jungle, unharmed and still strapped into her seat. She alone, of ninety-two passengers and crewmen, had survived the crash.

DANGLING FROM THE GOLDEN GATE BRIDGE AND OTHER NARROW ESCAPES

John Anthony Adams

BALLANTINE BOOKS • NEW YORK

Library of Congress Catalog Card Number: 88-91962

ISBN 0-345-34915-6

Printed in Canada

First Edition: September 1988

DEDICATION

Dedicated to my brother, James L. Adams, professor of mechanical engineering and chairman of the Values, Technology, Science, and Society Program at Stanford University as well as author of the best-selling book Conceptual Blockbusting, for encouraging me to become an author.

FOREWORD

I have long been fascinated by accounts of very unusual narrow escapes from such varied terrors as falling, crashes of aircraft and highway vehicles, drowning, earthquakes, towering tidal waves, forest fires, erupting volcanoes, tornadoes, lightning strikes, executions, bullets, artillery shells, bombs and other threats to life. However, I have never found a book in which the author tried to collect the most amazing narrow escapes ever recorded from a wide variety of very lethal dangers. This book was written in an attempt to do so.

The accounts of these seemingly miraculous survivals are interesting in themselves but it is also fascinating to explore why they were possible. How, for example, can a person survive a direct lightning strike, a ride in a tornado funnel, or fall for miles without a parachute and live to tell about it? The causes of very improbable narrow escapes will be discussed in the following chapters.

Another very interesting aspect of close brushes with death is that a survivor who has been saved at the last instant by some incredible, unexpected stroke of luck, can tell us much about what people experience in the moments before suffering such a death. For instance, a man who has fallen from a great height without a parachute toward apparently inevitable death can relate the sensations experienced in a fatal fall if, by some fluke, he lands in such a way that he survives. Survivor's recollections of their thoughts, emotions, and actions during narrow escapes are given in connection with many of the stories in this book.

Before beginning the book, I would like to express great appreciation to some who have given me vital help. Thanks to Charles Elliott, senior editor at Knopf, for sending the manuscript to Ballantine and thanks also to Chris Cox, editor at Ballantine, for showing so much interest in the book. I also greatly appreciate suggestions during the early stages of the manuscript from Jean Adams, my mother, from Professor James L. Adams of Stanford University, my brother, and from Marian Adams, my sister-in-law and head of Continuing Education at Stanford. Another family member who contributed essential help to the project was Sam Player, my nephew, who typed the entire manuscript with great accuracy.

CHAPTER I

Risky Encounters and Racing Minds

Are pilots headed for an apparently certain fatal crash gripped by numbing terror? Their minds are fully occupied with the desperate struggle for survival and if their efforts prove useless the final reaction, typically, is first frustration and then resignation. It is a well-known fact that the last spoken sounds on the cockpit recorder are not gasps or screams, but often—though always edited out in consideration of surviving family members—a bitter "Oh, shit!"

People who have narrowly missed death in accidents provide graphic accounts of the state of mind of a person who expects to be killed. Many are understandably terrified, but others report little fear, or even a feeling of great calm just before their expected death. One reason that many victims may not feel terror in rapidly developing accidents is that their aroused minds—concentrated on a desperate search for a means of survival and operating with enormously increased speed and clarity—simply do not permit terror or panic to enter the consciousness.

Albert von St. Gallem Heim, a geology professor at the University of Zurich, gave an account of his reactions during a potentially fatal fall in 1881.

"I fell between the front and rear wheels of a wagon

traveling between Aosta and St. Remy, and for a fleeting moment I was still able to hold on to the edge of the wagon. The following series of thoughts went through my mind: 'I cannot manage to hold on until the horse comes to a stop; I must let go. If I simply let go, I will fall on my back and the wheel will travel over my legs. Then at the least a fracture of the kneepan or shinbone will be unavoidable; I must fall upon my stomach and the wheel will pass over the backs of my legs. If I then tense the muscles, they will be a protective cushion for the bones. The pressure of the street will be somewhat less likely to break a bone than the pressure of the wheel. If I am able to turn myself to the left, then perhaps I can sufficiently draw back my left leg; on the other hand, turning to the right would, by the dimensions of the wagon, result in both legs being broken under it.' I know quite clearly that I let myself fall only after these lightning fast, wholly precise reflections, which seemed to imprint themselves upon my brain. Thereupon through a jerk of my arm, I turned myself to the left, swinging my leg powerfully outward, and simultaneously tensed my leg muscles to the limit of my strength. The wheel passed over my right ham, and I came out of it with a slight bruise. Several persons have told me quite similar stories. What they reveal is not merely an admirable presence of mind or a simple reflex movement. Much more than that they reflect the dread-endangered uttermost exertion of the human spirit appearing in moments of extreme excitement."

In a mind working in such a state, even if the victim can't save himself, there is no room for utter terror. Time becomes greatly expanded and the victim often takes a curiously detached view of things. But even though some people may be calm while surviving a great danger, they can be left shaking with terror afterward.

Reactions to narrow escapes

People's responses to near annihilation vary greatly. Some, with robust nervous systems, do not shy from danger despite repeated near disasters. Eddie Rickenbacker, the top-scoring American flying ace of World War I and later president of Eastern Airlines, counted 135 near brushes with death before he died peacefully at the age of eighty-two. He remembered as a child putting wings on a discarded bicycle, "flying" off the roof, and crashing. He kept piling up the string of close calls during his adventurous youth, while a leading automobile racer, during World Wars I and II, and through the intervening peacetime years. On one occasion during the Second World War, he crashed into the Pacific Ocean and survived twenty-one days on a raft before being rescued. No amount of potential calamity changed the risk-taking lifestyle of this indomitable man.

Some survivors attribute their escapes, perhaps unconsciously, to a kind of magic invincibility. They have a feeling of power over death and believe that "nothing can get me but a silver bullet."

Others, their brains perhaps rejecting the horrifying experience, have no memory of the traumatic incident even though they appeared fully conscious at the time. Some who have survived while others were killed may experience an irrational "survivor's guilt," in which they feel somehow responsible for the deaths of others or they may feel no more deserving of survival than those who were killed.

A person who survives a disaster may be brought face-to-face with his own mortality for the first time, especially with the possibility of the impending end of an unfulfilled life. Some regret the loss of their "innocence of death." Others remain forever "in thrall to their death encounter," and have a continued "fascination with scenes of death and devastation."*

Many of the stories you will read in this book actually are more improbable than those that could be used in any plausible fictional drama, although some might be appropriate in slapstick comedies. In the coming chapters we will examine the most extraordinary survivals of accidents;

*"Air Crash Survivors: The Troubled Aftermath," *Time* (15 January 1973): 53.

falls from great heights, including aircraft; near falls in which the unfortunate ones desperately held on for their own dear lives; crashes into all sorts of objects, mostly in airplanes but also in motor vehicles and even, in one case, a spacecraft; extraordinary avoidance of apparently inevitable crashes; ingenious escapes from sunken submarines and other submerged objects; surviving while overboard in the vastness of the seas; perilously riding on or being buried by avalanches; violent threats from earthquakes, volcanoes, and forest fires; living through lightning strikes; staying alive in tornado funnels; and survivals during the actual process of executions and from the impacts of bullets, shells, and bombs. We will see how such very unusual escapes were possible and learn what many of the victims experienced.

CHAPTER 2

Fearless Falling

Not being of a superstitious nature, Sgt. Nick Alkemade had no more than the normal fears of flying a wartime mission on his thirteenth raid over Berlin. The British bomber kept its steady course through the moon-brightened sky, dropped its bombs, and turned to fly away from the burning city. But March, 1944 was a very dangerous time to be a crewman in a British bomber. During the previous five months the constantly sharpening German antiaircraft defenses had hammered over one thousand English bombers out of the night skies.

Suddenly the crew members of Alkemade's bomber were made aware of the German fighter on their tail by the crashes of shells from winking cannons directed at them. One shell splintered and blew away the transparent blister covering Alkemade's tail turret, and he found himself staring directly out into space at the black fighter, its cannons still flashing. He fired his tail guns and watched the fighter plunge down into the night with one of its two engines a spurt of flame.

But his bomber was fatally stricken. Burning fuel whipped into the exposed turret as he desperately tried to shield his face with his arm. He heard the pilot's order to bail out and pushed open the tail turret doors to reach for his parachute pack on its rack at the back of the fuselage—kept there because there was no room to wear a parachute while squeezed into the narrow space of the tail turret. Alkemade saw his parachute wreathed in flames, the canopy case already blackening into ash. He realized that he was about to die, and the excruciating pain of the flames made it easy to choose the manner of his death. Better to die from a painless fall than from burning to death! He flung himself backward into space. The fall did not bring terror, but a feeling of great calm.

"I hadn't time to think—things had happened too swiftly. Less than a minute had elapsed since the Junkers 88 (the German nightfighter) set fire to our gas tanks. And now I was falling through space, more than eighteen thousand feet above Germany.

"I felt a strange peace away from that shriveling heat. As I plunged toward eternity I felt an enjoyment of the cool air rushing over my blistered face. I saw stars between my feet. Falling headfirst I thought casually. If this was dying it was nothing to be afraid of, only a pleasant experience. My only thoughts of an earthly nature were regrets over not saying good-bye to my friends. I was due for leave the following Sunday. It was a shame to miss that. I'd heard that a falling body reaches 120 mph. From eighteen thousand feet, I had ninety seconds to live. One minute and a half to bring to a close a very ordinary life.

"I blacked out. Awareness returned slowly—first as a point of light in a sea of darkness. I tried to think what it was. A star. I was cold, bitterly cold. My arms and legs felt paralyzed. I struggled to sit up. Then it came to me, with an overwhelming shock.

"'Jesus Christ, I'm alive!'

"This was no blasphemy, only a heartfelt prayer of thanksgiving. There had been a miracle, but my mind was still too numb to think on it. I ran my hands over my body and limbs, probing. I felt an agonizing pain in my back and shoulders. I was sore and stiff. My head throbbed. I identified each ache separately, and marveled that there were not more."

The fire in the bomber had burned Alkemade's face, hands, and legs, but he was in incredibly good shape for having fallen over three miles. A moderate concussion, bad scalp cut, strained back, twisted knee, and a deep splinter wound in his thigh were the extent of his injuries from the fall. He pulled matches and cigarettes out of his pocket, lit a match, and saw that he was lying in a snow bank. As he lay back in the snow, shakily puffing a cigarette, he saw the reason for his amazing survival. Above, the moonlight filtered down through the interlaced branches of tall fir trees which had slowed his fall, dropping him onto dense underbrush, which in turn cushioned him still further before his final stop on the snowbank.

Alkemade, his clothes in shreds and his flying boots lost, tried to stand up on legs that weren't cooperating. The cold was getting to him, and he decided that freezing to death would be worse than trying to get help, even though he would be a prisoner in enemy territory. Blowing the whistle attached to his tunic started some distant shouts, and soon a party of Germans found him, put him on a canvas, and dragged him to a nearby farmhouse. The kindly woman there gave him some strengthening eggnog while they waited for two Gestapo men to arrive. The men took him to a small hospital where doctors cut away his clothes and bathed him, and then to a private room for interrogation.

One of the Gestapo men asked Alkemade what he had done with his parachute. When he replied that he didn't have one—that he had jumped eighteen thousand feet without a chute—the unbelieving German lost his temper, slapped him across the face, and demanded to know where the English tail gunner had buried it. The interrogation continued for days, but the Germans never accepted his story.

After three weeks, Alkemade was taken to Dulag Luft, near Frankfurt, for final interrogation before going to a prisoner of war camp. He repeated his story and was summarily ordered into solitary confinement for a week to encourage him to come up with a more believable version of his arrival in Germany. Finally, in the middle of the night, he realized how to convince his captors he was telling the truth.

The next morning, when he was brought in front of Lt. Hans Feidal, a Luftwaffe officer, Alkemade said he could prove the story of his parachuteless jump if they would bring him the harness he had worn. This was done, and the officer was shown that the hooks and lift webs attached to the clips which should have held the chest canopy pack were still tied down with thread. If the chute had been used the threads would have broken as the lift webs were pulled free. Lieutenant Feidal turned the harness over and over with a look of astonishment as he realized the truth of the Englishman's claim.

Suddenly the German view of Alkemade made a right-angle turn, and from a despised POW he became a figure of awe. The German airmen were a tireless audience, urging him to tell and retell his story, laughing and congratulating him on being alive, and pressing on him rum, cigarettes, and candy. Arriving at the POW camp, Alkemade continued to receive celebrity treatment. Lieutenant Feidal requested the Senior Allied Officer to record for Sergeant Alkemade that his story had been investigated and found true. So Flight Lt. H. J. Moore tore a blank flyleaf from a Bible and wrote as Feidal dictated:

It has been investigated and corroborated by the German authorities that the claim of Sergeant Alkemade, No. 1431537 RAF, is true in all respects, namely, that he has made a descent from eighteen thousand feet without a parachute and made a safe landing without injuries, the parachute having been burnt in the aircraft. He landed in snow among young fir trees.

Corroboration witnessed by

Signed: F/Lt. H. J. Moore (SBO)
         F/S R. R. Lamb
         F/S T. A. Jones

Feeling "like a freak" in the POW camp and being the talk of the compound was not an all-bad experience, and Sgt. Alkemade was liberated in May 1945.

Alkemade welcomed the opportunity to return to a safer, duller life after the war, but he was to continue his series of dangerous escapades in peacetime. In 1946, shortly after demobilization, he started working in a chemical factory. One day he had to climb down into a pit to pump out a pool of liquid which was generating poisonous chlorine gas. After about half of the liquid had been removed, Alkemade received a severe electrical shock from the pump and, as the jolt staggered his body, the gas mask fell off his face. He was nearly asphyxiated by the time his fellow workers carried him out of the pit.

A few weeks later at the same factory, Alkemade was siphoning sulfuric acid when the pipe burst, drenching his face and arms with the acid. He might have been fatally burned except for a forty-gallon drum of limewash which was nearby. Alkemade immediately dived headfirst into the drum, neutralized the acid, and escaped with first degree burns. After recovering from the acid spill, Alkemade returned to the deadly factory only to be knocked flat by a nine-foot tall piece of steel which broke off and fell on top of him. The men who lifted the steel and pulled Alkemade out feared that he had been killed, but he was only bruised. Still, Alkemade had had enough of the chemical factory. He left to work as a furniture salesman.

Highest falls survived

Despite his enormous fall without a parachute, Alkemade does not hold the record for bailing out without a chute. I. M. Chisov of the USSR has been credited with an even longer free fall, in January 1942 when he fell from his severely damaged bomber. Falling 22,000 feet without a parachute, he was saved when he landed with a glancing blow on the side of a snow-covered ravine and slid to the bottom. He was more badly injured than Alkemade, with a fractured pelvis and severe spinal damage.

Even though Chisov fell from his plane four thousand feet higher than Alkemade, the two would probably have been traveling at about the same speed as they neared the ground. After about twelve seconds, a free-falling jumper reaches the point where the air resistance becomes equal to the force of gravity and he or she will fall no faster. After this length of time, the jumper will have fallen around fifteen hundred feet and will have reached a speed of about 120 mph (at normal atmospheric pressure) in a stable, spread-out position; or if falling head-downward, a speed of 185 mph.

At high altitudes, thin air allows much faster falls. Joseph Kittinger of the U.S. Air Force reached a maximum speed of 702 mph after he jumped from a balloon at an altitude of 102,800 feet. Kittinger was testing a multistage parachute that would allow someone bailing out at very high altitudes to make a stabilized descent down to ten thousand feet before opening the main parachute in an atmosphere with enough oxygen to sustain life. Tests with dummies had shown that in a descent from 83,000 feet, the body could spin up to 465 revolutions per minute—enough to cause not only loss of consciousness but even death. Of course, Kittinger slowed greatly in falling through increasingly denser air before opening his chute at 17,500 feet, after a fall of sixteen miles which had lasted for four minutes and thirty-seven seconds.

Sensations of falling

Falling through the air at a more normal 120 mph can be a very pleasant sensation. The following is a description by an early pioneer of free falling, Harry Armstrong, who jumped at twenty-two hundred feet and fell for twelve hundred feet—at a speed he later calculated as 119 mph—before pulling the ripcord:

"There was none of the empty or 'gone' feeling in the

abdomen so common in elevators and in airplanes. The eyes, although unprotected from the high wind blast, were not irritated. Breathing was even, regular, and undisturbed.

"The last phenomenon has to do with skin sensibility, and was a result of the air pressure on the lower surface of the body. It consists of that force which restricts terminal velocity to 119 mph instead of infinity, and appears in consciousness as a very gentle, evenly distributed, generalized, superficial pressure on the surface of the body toward the earth. The nearest possible similar earthly experience is that of being lowered gently into a giant bed of softest down."

Calm feelings recalled by fall survivors

In contrast to the euphoria experienced by a free-falling skydiver, who will open his chute and survive the fall, one would expect that the feeling of a free-falling victim who has no hope of survival by parachute would be of stark terror. Many of the thousands who die each year from falls must indeed have a feeling of horror; others, based on accounts of survivors such as Sergeant Alkemade, may feel calm while falling through great heights.

The earliest known study of the experiences of fall survivors was published in 1892 by Albert von St. Gallem Heim, the geology professor at the University of Zurich, whose fall under a wagon was described in Chapter One. His "Remarks on Fatal Falls," was based on twenty-five years of experience in the mountains and on hundreds of interviews with climbers, roofers, and assorted accident victims who had survived falls. His conclusion was that most fall victims do not suffer greatly.

"The subjective perceptions of those who fall to their deaths are the same whether they fall from the scaffolding of a house or the face of a cliff." Heim concluded that his survivors "awoke as though from death and could tell us exactly what those who have actually died from sudden misfortune must have experienced."

In nearly ninety-five percent of his interviews he found that "no grief was felt nor was there paralyzing fright of the sort that can happen in instances of lesser danger (e.g., outbreak of fire). There was no anxiety, no trace of despair, no pain, but rather calm seriousness, profound acceptance, and a dominant mental quickness and sense of surety. Mental activity became enormous, rising to a hundredfold velocity or intensity. The relationships of events and their probable outcomes were overviewed with objective clarity. No confusion entered at all. Time became greatly expanded. The individual acted with lightning quickness in accord with accurate judgment of his situation. In many cases there followed a sudden review of the individual's entire past; and, finally, the person falling often heard beautiful music and fell in a superbly blue heaven containing roseate cloudlets. Then consciousness was painlessly extinguished, usually at the moment of impact, and the impact was, at the most, heard but never painfully felt. Apparently hearing is the last of the senses to be extinguished."

Except for the claim of "hearing beautiful music" while falling, these generalizations coincide with many of the accounts of falls that I have collected—some of which will be presented in the remainder of this chapter.

A good example of a mountain climber's reaction to a fall was reported by Edward Whymper, one of the greatest figures in climbing history. In 1865 Whymper's party of seven climbers was the first to reach the top of the Matterhorn, and after this great triumph, while descending the mountain, four of the seven climbers fell to their death as Whymper and two other survivors watched in horror. However, the fall described by Whymper was one he had himself suffered in 1862 while climbing alone on the Matterhorn. He fell two hundred feet down a very steep gully striking ice and rocks seven or eight times on the way down and finally stopping ten feet from the edge of a precipice that would have dropped him onto a glacier eight hundred feet below. Whymper wrote:

"As it seldom happens that one survives such a fall, it

may be interesting to record what my sensations were during its occurrence. I was perfectly conscious of what was happening, and felt each blow, but like a patient under chloroform, experienced no pain. Each blow was, naturally, more severe than that which preceded it, and I distinctly remember thinking, 'Well, if the next is harder still, that will be the end!' Like persons who have been rescued from drowning, I remember that the recollection of a multitude of things rushed through my head, many of them trivialities or absurdities which had been forgotten long before; and more remarkable, this bounding through space did not feel disagreeable. But I think that in not very great distance, more consciousness as well as sensation would have been lost, and upon those I base my belief, improbable as it seems, that death by a fall from a great height is as painless an end as can be experienced."

Often the fall appears to be more horrifying to a faller's companion than to the faller. Professor Heim, who himself had a fall at sixty six feet, wrote that, "Often the spectator, incapacitated by paralyzing horror and quaking in body and soul, carries away from the experience a lasting trauma. I must even testify that the memory of a cow's fall is still painful for me, while my own misfortune is registered as a pleasant transfiguration."

In the early days of parachuting there were arguments about how far a chutist could tumble down through the sky in a free fall before opening his chute. Some people thought that a jumper could keep full control of his senses from any height and survive, whereas others thought he would eventually lose consciousness and plunge to his death. In 1919 a Royal Air Force officer's chute fouled on bailout, and he was seen to kick and claw at the air until he hit the ground. Undoubtedly an example of a man who didn't enjoy the fall. This incident gave rise to the saying "It isn't the fall that kills you. It's the landing!" However, even though we know that humans have remained conscious in free falls as long as sixteen miles, a faller may lose consciousness immediately.

Professor Heim wrote that some fallers lose consciousness at the start of a fall, and it has been speculated that a person might even die of fright at the beginning of a fall. The first reaction to falling might cause the heart rate first to rise and then to drop tremendously (this is called "the diving reflex"). A faller could lose enough blood flow to the brain to cause him to lose consciousness, and cardiac arrest could follow.

CHAPTER 3

Falling Onto All Sorts of Things

N ow that we have seen some aspects of falling and its possible effects on the victim's state of mind, let's look at an extremely important subject for the survivors of very high falls: the types of surfaces that they have landed on to save them. Alkemade and Chisov survived falls from aircraft as a result of freakish landings involving snow and being slowed before their falls came to an end, but some fallers from aircraft have survived landings directly onto soft ground.

The list of hospitable landing sites that have saved falling humans is highly varied. In a Wright-brothers–type plane being flown over Staten Island, New York, in 1913, Arthur Lapham fell from his precarious perch on the wing. After falling feet first for three hundred feet he found himself buried up to his armpits, but uninjured, in mud of the salt flats near Prince's Bay.

Another man fell 150 feet from the scaffold of a large smokestack into loose rubble on a 30-degree slope where he landed on his side, making a depression eight inches deep. He then bounced and rolled over a concrete retaining wall. Finally he dropped another ten feet to a lower level, where he was found by some horrified "sidewalk superintendents." He had a fracture of the left ankle and a chip fracture of the other, a linear fracture of the left lower jaw, and complained of chest pains for a couple of days. His recovery was rapid. Scientists at Cornell University, studying the accident to better learn the tolerance of human beings to crash forces, particularly in relation to crash landings of manned space vehicles, concluded that the man survived an estimated 162 Gs (one G being equal to the acceleration of gravity) when his body hit the ground. This force is sufficient to totally demolish virtually any aircraft in existence.

A well-executed and coordinated escape from a fall occurred at a building construction site. High above the street a riveter was sitting on a newly riveted steel girder attached to the frame. As he was lighting a cigarette, the girder came loose and dropped with him toward the ground. His companions, thinking him doomed, watched unbelievingly as he jumped from the girder and landed on a canvas canopy stretched over some building material as the girder buried itself in the ground. The riveter was taken to the hospital but suffered only shock and bruises.

Canvas also saved a student who fell nine stories from a residence hall at the University of California at Berkeley in 1986. The nineteen-year-old-student suffered only minor cuts and bruises when he landed on the canvas sunroof of a parked car, ripped through the canvas, and came to rest on the car's seat cushions. Another student who ran to the parking lot to aid the stunned young man found him asking where he was and what had happened. Fellow students said the young man liked to sit on the window ledge of his room and apparently had lost his balance.

Falling out of and back onto airplanes

Some of the truly incredible survivals of falls have occurred after men have fallen out of airplanes only to land back on their own airplanes or on another airplane.

Falls from planes were, of course, much more common in the old days of open cockpits and wingwalkers. Many pioneering fliers scorned safety belts, and rough air could easily throw a pilot or passenger from the plane. For example, one of the early U.S. Navy pilots, Ens. William D. Billingsly, fell to his death in rough air from a Wright float plane at sixteen hundred feet, while his passenger, Lt. John H. Towers, who later became a vice admiral, saved himself by clutching to a strut as the plane crash-landed itself.

In 1917 Lieutenant Bohrle of the German Air Force, riding as an observer over the French lines in World War I, was hurled out of the airplane at thirteen thousand feet when its engine suddenly stopped. As the plane plunged down, its pilot, Lieutenant Rosengart, felt a bump and discovered that Bohrle had landed back in his own seat. Rosengart managed to restart the engine and they landed safely behind their own lines.

In 1918, while attempting to dodge German gunfire, a Canadian pilot named Makepiece went into a sharp dive and his observer, Capt. J. H. Sedley, fell out of the plane. When Makepiece leveled off several hundred feet below, Sedley landed on the tail of the airplane. Sedley clung to the tail, then crawled into his seat unharmed. The plane finally landed safely behind Allied lines.

Marty Jensen and his passenger, a young ensign learning to fly, were both wearing seat belts as they flew over San Diego in 1925. The ensign, in the rear seat, was supposed to put the plane into a spin by easing the control stick forward. Instead he shoved it full forward and as the plane dove beneath, both men were thrown upward with such force that their seat belts snapped. The ensign was thrown clear, but Jensen, hurled against the top of the fuselage, managed to hold onto the control stick and then pull back on it, bringing the plane out of its dive. The ensign, falling earthward, landed just forward of the tail on top of the fuselage of the plane, causing the plane to zoom up again. He had punched a hole in the top of the fuselage when he crashed into it,

so he rode safely to a landing seated in this new opening. In 1976, when Jensen told this story on television,
an excited S. L. Potter of Alpine, California, called Jensen to say that he had seen it all from the ground fifty-
one years before. Another fuselage rider was a student
pilot who was bounced out of his plane by a downdraft
in 1941 over St. Louis. He hung on to the rear part of
the plane riding backward like a frightened jockey while
the instructor did a fine job of landing gently.

Aviation Cadet Derek M. Sharp fell from the cockpit of
a plane five hundred feet above the ground. As he flew
backward he felt something bump his head. Instinctively
he raised his arms and felt himself hugging the tail of his
own plane. He managed to pull himself up on the plane's
elevator surfaces, which made the airplane bounce. When
the pilot saw the reason for his plane's erratic progress
through the air he made a quick landing and Cadet Sharp
climbed down from the tail unhurt.

People have also fallen out of more modern planes
with enclosed cockpits and managed to get back in. The
National Safety Council listed a freak accident in 1952 in
which an Air Force captain from Dallas, Texas, wearing
a parachute, accidentally fell out of the door of a C-46
twin-engine propeller-driven cargo plane. It was flying a
mile high over Korea during the Korean war. Just as he
was about to pull the ripcord of his parachute, the plane
hit a downdraft, and the captain flew back into the plane
through the same door by which he had so recently left.

Less common are accidents where someone has fallen
from an airplane and safely come to rest on a second airplane. One such incident involved a great movie stunt
pilot, Frank Clarke. A man named Al Wilson was hanging
by his knees without a parachute from the wing skid of a
biplane as Clarke flew up from behind to pick him off in a
plane-change stunt. Before Clarke had reached the position
for the transfer he saw Wilson beginning to slip. Just as
Wilson lost his grip and began to fall, Clarke dove at full
power beneath Wilson's falling body, and after a fall estimated to be about fifty feet, Wilson ripped head first

through Clarke's upper wing and stuck there, five thousand feet above the ground. Clarke gingerly returned to earth with the bruised but very lucky Wilson still lodged in his wing.

Landing on things attached to their bodies

Another very intriguing category of survivors of free falls are those whose impact with the ground was softened by some object strapped to their bodies, such as an airline seat or a backpack. A delicate looking seventeen-year-old girl, who fell from an exploded airliner over the Peruvian jungle in 1971 while still strapped to her airline seat, would make anyone's list of improbably lucky people. Juliane Koepcke, newly graduated from a high school in Lima, was traveling with her mother to spend Christmas with both parents at their remote home in the jungle. Juliane was sitting in a window seat next to her mother as the pilot asked the passengers to fasten their seat belts for the landing.

Suddenly the airliner was engulfed in a violent jungle storm. Juliane saw a brilliant flash, and flames tore over the right wing. Horrified, she looked at her mother who said, "This is the end of everything." That was the last Juliane ever saw of her.

Juliane felt herself twisting and whirling as she fell through the air, still strapped in her seat. Her next memory was the sound of jungle birds as she found herself lying on the shaded floor of the dense jungle, with the seat she was in attached to two empty ones. She alone, of ninety-two passengers and crewmen, had survived.

Anyone falling while strapped to an airline seat is likely to tumble end-over-end—in contrast to the stable position maintained by someone falling with head thrust back and limbs outstretched. For this reason crewmen ejecting from disabled aircraft usually are separated by an automatic release from their seats one or two seconds after being blown out of the cockpit. However, miraculously, Juliane was not only safely flung away from the fragments of the disintegrating aircraft, but survived a spinning fall in her seat, which became properly oriented when hitting the thick tree canopy so that she could be slowed and dropped to safety on the ground below.

Shocked but still clearheaded, Juliane got out of her seat and began to walk around, looking for her mother or other survivors. She was in remarkably good condition, with only a broken collar bone and cut upper right arm to show for her appalling drop from the skies. She was wearing a frilly dress and white high-heeled shoes and her vision was blurry because her glasses had disappeared during the fall. She ate some small Christmas cakes she found on the jungle floor (they had also fallen from the plane), and later regretted discarding one that was wet, as she was to go many days without food.

She spent the night huddled under the airplane seat to protect herself from chilling rains, and the next day began a long trek through the jungle. She shuddered as she passed a section of three inverted seats attached to the bodies of three teen-aged girls.

She had spent much of her childhood in the jungle with her parents—both German-born biologists who studied Peruvian animals. Her father had always told her to walk downhill, if lost, until she found water, and then follow the water downstream to an inhabited area. As Juliane struggled through the jungle her high-heeled shoes were soon abandoned and her dress was shredded. Finally she found a thatched lean-to on the riverbank and she stayed there, too exhausted to walk any farther. After three days some hunters floated by in a canoe. The superstitious natives thought the blond girl might be an evil spirit, but after a while they came ashore and gave her food. They cleaned the jungle worms from her skin with gasoline, then took her down the river to a doctor. Eleven days after she fell into the jungle she was reunited with her distraught father.

Another extraordinary case of salvation by an aircraft seat took place in 1954. Flying officer Peter Underdown of the Royal Air Force took off in a jet fighter from a German airbase and climbed westward across the Dutch-German border into Holland. Then, astonishingly, he was aware that he was lying in a hospital bed. His ribs were sore and he couldn't see properly from his right eye, but otherwise he felt all right. The shocked Underdown demanded to know why he was in a hospital and what day it was. The Dutch doctor told him that his airplane exploded and that he had been found, still strapped to his aircraft seat, in a tree—three days earlier.

Later in the day, some RAF officers came to visit him. They told him that his plane had disintegrated two minutes after takeoff, and they asked him questions about what might have caused the breakup of the aircraft. But Underdown couldn't help them. He remembered events earlier in the day of his flight, but he didn't remember any crash or landing in a tree.

A large number of Dutch people in a nearby village had seen the crash, and with their help, the very improbable story of Underdown's crash was pieced together. They had seen the plane pitch steeply, first up, then down. Flames had spurted out of one wing root, both wings folded upward, and then a series of explosions left only a mass of wreckage flying through the air two thousand feet above the ground where the fighter had been.

Among the flying wreckage was Underdown, still strapped in his ejection seat. The breakup had come so quickly that he had no time to eject. As the plane's nose pitched violently down, the seat had torn loose and ripped out through the jet fighter's plastic hood. The ejection seat had no stabilizing drogue chute to slow it down, and Underdown never pulled the ripcord of his own parachute, so the seat shot away from the cockpit at 400 mph and tore through the sky over a long arc. The villagers watched it curve forward ahead of the main debris and then disappear behind a tree-covered slope.

A short time later a Dutch policeman found the seat perched in an apple tree, a few feet above the ground. He was amazed to find the man not only alive, but shouting. Within a half hour Underdown was in a hospital, still apparently conscious and still talking, although somewhat incoherently. The doctors expected to find, at the very least, serious internal injuries, but his only injuries were a mild concussion, bruises, five broken ribs, a dislocated shoulder, a strained right eye muscle, and a fracture of one of the smaller pelvis bones. Four weeks later he was out of the hospital, still with no memory of his accident.

Underdown had been saved by a lucky combination of factors. The seat, in its spinning flight, had hurtled into an apple orchard and hit the first tree backward, thus protecting him with the metal structure behind him. The trees were on a sloping angle and the seat's trajectory coincided with the angle of the slope—about ten feet above the ground—ripping through tree after tree until it slowed enough to come to rest in the stout fork of an apple tree. .

He never regained any recollection of his three-day memory gap. Investigating officers even hypnotized him in an attempt to restore his memory of the accident, but he only recovered an additional half hour of memory recollection—up to the point of his take-off, but not the crash. He may have been unconscious after the breakup started, but he was conscious and speaking when found in the apple tree and later in the hospital.

Why did Underdown have no memories of this time? Sometimes the shock of a sudden catastrophe may cause victims to forget past incidents. For example, after a jetliner crash in Florida, a passenger reported that "My wife tells me she unfastened my seat belt and we walked to a group of people who seemed in fairly good condition. I have no recollection of this." Underdown's stunned mind may have similarly erased his own memories.

Could wearing a backpack save your life in a fall? If one wouldn't, two did in the case of a doctor serving an Italian regiment during World War II. The doctor, acting the part of the good samaritan, had picked up the pack of an exhausted soldier in mountainous country and hitched it to his own while edging along a narrow ledge with only open space below. He slipped at the worst possible moment, and soon his hands were where his feet had been, and his fingers were desperately gripping the ledge. He called for help but the soldier stood paralyzed by fear. The doctor's hands could hold no more and he fell away into the air. He later reported a strange reaction:

"Holding nothing, by nothing withheld, I rested for a moment in the abyss, as in bed. After the effort to hang on, it was restful. I don't think I have ever been or shall ever be again as comfortable as I was at that moment. I have never known such abandonment."

The knapsacks saved him when he landed on them—as on a rounded soft hump—on an inclined rocky slope thirty feet below the ledge. He rolled down at least another thirty feet and stopped amid a heavy growth of heather, in great pain but able to walk with help down to his base. He told of the after effects:

"I suffered no long-lasting damage other than dreams. Often I have dreams about it. In them I don't rest, but twist and writhe in the abyss and never come to the bottom. They end only when I awake. Then I sit up on my bed, afraid to go to sleep again, and wonder why the dreams should be worse than the reality—why when it happened, the air should have been like the softest bed I have known, and why, in my dreams, a bottomless pit."

Later he went to New York City for a visit. While walking in the rain with his umbrella he observed the massive, many-terraced skyscrapers, which reminded him of mountain cliffs he had seen. Afterward, lying in bed and recapturing the feelings of his fall, he went to sleep and dreamed again of the mountain fall, but in a very different way:

"I did dream. I was in midair, but not writhing and twisting; an umbrella was breaking my fall. With the slowness and lightness of a soap bubble, I sank down the side of the cliff past pretty crannies and nooks, past edelweiss that not even the boldest and most expert climber would have been able to reach, and landed as softly as a leaf."

This was such a captivating dream in contrast to his former nightmares that he wished for another such dream. But he had no more about his fall. He concluded that, perhaps, his wish for dreams had kept them away.

High falls into water

Now let's talk about diving and falls from great heights into water, and compare the progressive perils. Dives from a height of ten meters (thirty-three feet) seem terrifying to most people. A high diver falling from this height enters the water at a speed of around 30 mph. The highest regularly performed dive into water is made by professional divers from La Quevrada ("the break in the rocks") at Acapulco, Mexico, a height of 118 feet. The base rocks are twenty-one feet out from the takeoff, and divers must leap out twenty-seven feet, hitting the water at a whistling 57 mph. Some divers have made this dive tens of thousands of times.

In March 1974, Donnie Vick, Pat Sucher, and John Tobler dove 130 feet, 6 inches into water on the "Wide World of Sports" television program. A diver jumping from this height takes three seconds to hit the water. The fall from the Golden Gate Bridge in San Francisco, from a height of 220 feet, takes about four seconds, and that extra second adds so much energy to the fall that it almost always proves fatal. The bridge jumpers hit the water at about 80 mph, and only 22 out of 801 suicide jumpers have survived the fall.

The first survivor of the fall (in 1941) from the Golden Gate Bridge was Cornelia Van Ierland, an attractive twenty-two-year-old brunette, who was engaged to be married. Afterward she told of her experience:

"I don't know what happened. I had an irresistible impulse to jump, and suddenly I clambered over the railing and fell into space. I had no particular sensation going down. I know I prayed, but I had no feeling of pressure against me, no sensation of falling. I don't remember when I hit the water, but I know I was conscious. I was conscious every moment."

Painters working on the bridge heard her scream during her four-second fall. After being alerted, coast guardsmen drifted under the bridge ready to pick up the body of another suicide. They were startled to hear faint cries for help. As they lifted the woman out of the water seven minutes after she had jumped, she was calm and smiled wanly. However, later, at the hospital she became distraught and hysterical. Cornelia Van Ierland's silk stockings were shredded, her shoes had torn off, and her clothes had been ripped by the force of the impact. Both of her arms were broken, vertebrae were fractured in her back and neck, and the flesh on her legs and thighs was badly bruised and torn. California officials, anxious for her welfare, urged that her serviceman fiance be released from the service in order to be able to marry and care for the injured woman. He was released (three days before the Pearl Harbor attack), and they were married in March 1942.

A few fortunate people have survived falls from bridges even higher than the Golden Gate. In 1968 Jeffry Kramer, twenty-four, leaped off the George Washington Bridge, 250 feet above the Hudson River, New York City, and survived. In 1885 Sarah Ann Henley, also twenty-four, jumped from the Clifton Suspension Bridge, 250 feet above the Avon in England. Her voluminous dress and petticoat acted as a small parachute, and she landed, bruised and bedraggled, in the riverbank mud. She was carried away to a hospital by policemen.

Some very precarious escapes when diving into water have been from lesser heights than the high bridges. Some apparently fatal falls have been survived when the victim landed in a small pool of water. For example, in June 1985, a teenage boy, climbing on a vertical cliff in the San Gabriel Mountains of California, lost his grip and hurtled downward toward the ground 150 feet below.

He landed in a pool of water, formed from mountain runoff, which was four feet deep, six feet wide, and eight feet long. He suffered a cut knee and some bruises and was released from a hospital after treatment of his injuries.

A classic survival story involved a fall into water from a height of 162 feet. This happened when Roger Woodward, a seven-year-old boy, was swept over Niagara Falls wearing only a life jacket. Ten daredevils have attempted to survive the plunge over the falls—protected in barrels or other containers—and seven have lived and three have died. Roger didn't intend to top their stunts when he went boating in 1960 with his sister and a family friend seven hundred yards from the falls. However, the motor cut out; the boat was swamped by a wave, and all three were soon rushing toward the precipice of Horseshoe Falls. Roger's sister was pulled out by tourists as she came close to shore a few yards from the edge, but Roger and the family friend went over. "I turned in the air," Roger recalled. "There was a lot of noise . . . I hit the bottom and came to the top." How did Roger do it? He weighed only fifty-five pounds, rode the surface of the falls, was cushioned by his life jacket and the foam at the bottom of the falls, and most importantly, sheer luck landed him in a spot free of big boulders. Some sharp-eyed men on a tourist boat saw Roger in the water below the falls and pulled him out less than ten minutes after he had first fallen into the river. He was hospitalized for slight cuts and bruises but quickly recovered. "I went over the falls," Roger said. "I really did!" The family friend who had also gone over the falls came to a more likely fate—he was found below the falls, crushed.

One whose life was spared in a fall into water from a much greater height than a bridge or waterfall was Lt. Cliff Judkins, a navy pilot making a transatlantic flight, who was forced to bail out of a burning fighter over the ocean. His ejection seat didn't work so he had to crawl out over the side. He missed the knife-edged wing and tail surface, but when he pulled his ripcord at ten thousand feet, the chute only streamed—it did not open. He fell for two miles and smashed into the ocean so hard that when he was rescued his face "resembled ten pounds of overripe calf's liver" and his ankles "looked like two broken flower pots." His chances of survival looked very poor when he was first rescued, but he lived to fly again. His remarkable recovery might have depended on an unusual circumstance. He was the only pilot in the squadron without a spleen, the organ which often ruptures in a hard fall, and almost always causes fatal hemorrhaging.

CHAPTER 4

Hanging On

One of the most famous and memorable scenes in historical movies is Harold Lloyd dangling from a clock hand high above Los Angeles, with the hand threatening to give way at any minute—when suddenly the whole clockworks pop out of their case, sprouting springs and gears. Can we find similar predicaments in real life which equal or top this vivid image from the greatest of all thrill movies, "Safety Last"?

Let's try the case of S. Hall Young, with both arms paralyzed and slipping over the edge of a thousand foot sheer drop, with only his chin to hold him back. Young had come to Alaska in 1878, fresh from a seminary, to work as a missionary among the Thlinget Indians. The next year he was invited by John Muir, the famous naturalist and conservationist, to join him in climbing an Alaskan peak. Muir, a man of enormous enthusiasm and stamina, was determined to reach the top in time to see the sunset. The climb was a perilous one, across deep crevasses of glaciers and then up a thousand feet of sheer rock face, all without ropes or other climbing equipment.

By the time the two climbers neared the top, Young was exhausted and struggling to keep the fast-moving

Muir in sight. As Young climbed up along a narrow
shelf, only forty or fifty feet from the top, he came to a
gap in the path about five feet wide which opened unto a
steep, gravel-covered slope. Twelve feet below, the slope
dropped off a thousand feet to a glacier at the bottom of
the cliff. His strength ebbing and muscles twitching, he
grew careless and stepped on a rock which projected
from the gravel to help get across. The rock gave way at
once and Young shot with it down toward the precipice.
Ten years before he had fallen several times, while
breaking and training horses, and dislocated first one
shoulder and then the other. After that, additional accidents had wrenched each of his arms out of joint more
than once. Now he had to use these weakened arms to
grasp the rocks on the sides of the fissure in a desperate
attempt to stop his fall. His hands struck the walls with a
stunning blow and both of his shoulders were instantly
dislocated. With his paralyzed arms flopping helplessly
above his head he dug his toes and chin into the gravel
to slow his deadly slide, but he could stop only when his
feet hung out over the edge of the cliff. Even then he
dared not move a muscle, so tenuous was his position.
He seemed to be slipping inch by inch to the point where
all would give way, and he would plummet to certain
death on the waiting glacier below.

His mind began to race at lightning speed:

"After the first wild moment of panic when I felt myself falling, I do not remember any sense of fear. But I
know what it is to have a thousand thoughts flash
through the brain in a single instant—an anguished
thought of my young wife at Wrangell, with her imminent motherhood; an indignant thought of the insurance
companies that refused me policies on my life; a thought
of wonder as to what would become of my poor flocks
of Indians among the islands; recollections of events far
and near in time—each thought printed upon my memory by the instantaneous photography of deadly peril. I
had no hope of escape at all. The gravel was rattling past
me and piling up against my head. The jar of a little

rock, and all would be over. The situation was too desperate for actual fear. Dull wonder as to how long I would be in the air, and the hope that death would be instant—that was all. Then came the wish that Muir would come before I fell, and take a message to my wife."

At that moment Young heard Muir's voice above him. "My God!" he exclaimed, assessing the situation. "Grab that rock, man, just by your right hand." Young gurgled out a reply from his throat, not daring to inflate his lungs: "My arms are out." Muir replied, "Hold fast! I'm going to get you out of this. I can't get to you on this side, the rock is sheer. I'll have to leave you now and cross the rift high up and come to you on the other side by which we came. Keep cool."

Young didn't understand how Muir could possibly rescue him, but he still felt better, having watched Muir's powerful climbing all day. Although it seemed hours for the suffering Young, Muir returned ten minutes later. By then the slowly slipping man hung so far over the precipice that he felt his remaining life span could be measured in seconds.

Muir had worked his way down the slope to a point below and behind Young, with his feet on a tiny, narrow, ridgelike ledge. He grabbed the back of the shirt, vest, and waistband of the pants of the stranded climber with one hand and clutched a small rock spur with his other. "Now!" he said, and Young slid down out of the cleft and his feet came against the cliff. "Work downward with your feet," Muir told him, and Young's feet stopped against the little ledge. Muir bit into Young's collar, as his teeth were the only way to tighten his grasp. "I've got to let go of you," Muir hissed through his teeth. "I need both hands here. Climb upward with your feet."

Young was never to get over his amazement at what happened next:

"How he did it, I know not. The miracle grows as I ponder it. The wall was almost perpendicular and smooth. My weight on his jaws dragged him outward.

And yet, holding me by his teeth as a panther her cub and clinging like a squirrel to a tree, he climbed with me straight up ten or twelve feet, with only the help of my feet scrambling on the rock. It was utterly impossible, yet he did it!

"When he landed me on the little shelf along which we had come, my nerves gave way and I trembled all over. I sank down exhausted, Muir no less tired, but supporting me."

On the terrifying trip down the thousand feet of sheer rock, Muir sometimes carried Young on his back, at other times swung him by the wrist to lower shelves of rock, and sometimes climbed below him and allowed him to fall against his rescuer and be eased down to Muir's standing ground.

It was dark and moonless when they finally reached the glacier. As it would be impossible to get across the crevasses, they solved the problem by going around it, sliding for a half mile in the loose gravel which the receding glacier had deposited. After another struggle down a steep canyon, they reached safety in the early light of the next day.

Muir's relish for dangerous climbs, often without a companion, caused him to have quite a few exciting escapades; in a later chapter we will see his enthusiastic account of a ride on an avalanche. One of his closest and most unusual brushes with death occurred after he crept out on a precarious perch, high up on a vertical rock face, to have a nighttime view of the moon through Yosemite Falls. Muir enjoyed the sight of the moon's light passing through the fall's filmy border, and when the wind swayed the water away from the cliff, Muir moved further along the cliff to see how the moon would look through the denser parts of the fall:

"The effect was enchanting: fine, savage music sounding above, beneath, around me; while the moon, apparently in the very midst of the rushing waters, seemed to be struggling to keep her place, on account of the ever-varying form and density of the water masses through which she was seen, now darkly veiled or eclipsed by a rush of thickheaded comets, now flashing out through openings between their tails."

However, Muir overlooked what would happen when the wind pressure was removed and the fall shifted back toward the cliff.

"Down came a splash of spent comets, thin and harmless-looking in the distance, but they felt desperately solid and stony when they struck my shoulders, like a mixture of choking spray and gravel and big hailstones. Instinctively dropping on my knees, I gripped an angle of the rock, curled up like a young fern frond with my face pressed against my breast, and in this attitude submitted as best I could to my thundering bath. The heavier masses seemed to strike like cobblestones, and there was a confused noise of many waters around my ears—hissing, gurgling, clashing sounds that were not heard as music. The situation was quickly realized. How fast one's thoughts burn in such times of stress! I was weighing chances of escape. Would the column be swayed a few inches away from the wall, or would it come yet closer? The fall was in flood and not so lightly would its ponderous mass be moved. My fate seemed to depend on a breath of the 'idle wind.' It was moved gently forward, the pounding ceased, and I was once more visited by glimpses of the moon."

After the frightening danger of being whisked off the cliff by the waterfall to a crushing death on the rocks below, Muir retreated from the rock face, "somewhat nerve-shaken, drenched, and benumbed." After warming himself by a fire and sleeping for an hour or two, Muir awoke "sound and comfortable. Better, not worse, for my hard, midnight bath."

John Muir wrote a revealing account of how his mind and body reacted to extreme danger, based on another risky incident while climbing a very steep slope high above a glacier in the Sierra Nevada Mountains of California:

"After gaining a point about halfway to the top, I was

suddenly brought to a dead stop, with arms outspread, clinging to the face of the rock, unable to move hand or foot either up or down. My doom appeared fixed. I *must* fall. There would be a moment of bewilderment, and then a lifeless tumble down the one general precipice to the glacier below.

"When this final danger flashed upon me, I became nerve-shaken for the first time since setting foot on the mountains, and my mind seemed to fill with a stifling smoke. But this terrible eclipse lasted only a moment, when life blazed forth again with preternatural clearness. I seemed suddenly to become possessed of a new sense. The other self, bygone experiences, instinct, or Guardian Angel—call it what you will—came forward and assumed control. Then my trembling muscles became firm again, every rift and flaw in the rock was seen as through a microscope, and my limbs moved with a positiveness and precision with which I seemed to have nothing at all to do. Had I been borne upon wings, my deliverance could not have been more complete."

The extreme exertion of mind and body which comes forth at times of great peril is so powerful that it may even obliterate a suicidal intent.

Dangling under the Golden Gate Bridge

An exceptionally pretty twenty-two-year-old girl was driving across San Francisco's Golden Gate Bridge in her Thunderbird in 1960. Her beauty had won for her such titles as "Candy Queen," "Sugar Beet Queen," and "Fiesta Dream Girl," but she felt very depressed about her life at the time, so she stopped her car, ran to the rail in her three-inch heels, and jumped over the side. Passing motorists reported her jump and coast guardsmen searched below the bridge for two hours without finding her body. Then a patrolman looked over a rail and was amazed to see her crawling along a girder. She was stunned and incoherent and couldn't tell her story until the next day.

"Somehow my heel caught in the bridge railing. I fell but not straight down. The next thing I know, I was hanging onto the cable for dear life. I was panicky, I didn't want to fall, so I just inched my way along a steel beam. I must have walked the length of the bridge before I got up again near the tollgate."

She was taken to a hospital for an overnight psychiatric examination. "But I didn't need it," she said. "Believe me, I wanted to live!"

Hanging from a dirigible cable

A dangle which might be the greatest of all dangles took place not from a mountain or bridge, but from a dirigible, the U.S. Navy's *Akron*, in 1931. Bud Cowart, a rugged, twenty-one-year-old sailor, was pulling with other crewmen on ropes to help bring the dirigible in for a landing at Camp Kearney, near San Diego. Heat from the sun and the ground quickly expanded the *Akron*'s helium, making the dirigible extremely buoyant. The *Akron*'s nose bobbed up and the men on the forward ropes were lifted slightly off the ground. Then the tail floated up, nearly standing the big airship on her nose. Lt. Commander Charles E. Rosendahl, the ship's captain, gave orders to vent helium, but it was too late. "Cut the mooring cable!" he ordered. "Let everything go!"

The cable attached to the mast was released and the ground crewmen were told to let go of their ropes. The *Akron* shot into the air, but three men were still clinging to the ropes. One fell from fifty feet above the ground and the second slipped off from one hundred feet even before the first man had hit the ground. A mechanic on the dirigible watched as the second man hit and bounced. "My God!" he said to his partner. "That kid smoked when he hit the ground." Both men were dead.

Bud Cowart, the last man remaining on the rope, hung

on, sitting astride one of the rods extended through the rope to provide a grip for the ground crewmen. Captain Rosendahl knew that if he tried to land the buoyant airship he would probably dash the sailor to death. The captain ordered the rudder man to head for the ocean where the air was smoother.

The sailor, dangling hundreds of feet below the airship, was now two thousand feet above the Pacific. "Hey!" he yelled, "when the hell are you going to land me?"

The men in the *Akron* were trying to figure out a way to haul Cowart up into the ship. The cable which attached the airship to the mooring mast had a winch that might be used to wind up the hundreds of feet of rope attached to him, *but the top twenty-five feet of the ground-crew line was one-inch steel cable*, which was too big to revolve around the drum of the mooring winch.

Boatswain's Mate Second Class Dick Deal volunteered to go down and tie a line below the steel cable section of the ground-crew line. Deal was slowly lowered out of the nose of the dirigible in a bosun's chair. Swaying dangerously, twenty-five feet below the bow platform, he grabbed for the ground-crew line on which Cowart was hanging. Finally he reached it and managed to tie a line to it. Then the steel cable section was cut off and the ground crew line was attached to the mooring winch.

Cowart held on to his precarious perch on the rope as he was cranked up into the dirigible a few feet at a time—it took an hour and a half—until he could be hoisted up to the bow platform. A crewman reached out and pulled him to safety. He looked around curiously—he had never been in a dirigible before.

"Son," Captain Rosendahl asked him, "what did you think of your ride?"

"Captain," Cowart answered with a grin, "that was a lily dilly!"

As fortunate as Cowart was, Dick Deal, who tied the line to Cowart's rope, was even luckier—he survived a series of dirigible disasters. He had been tagged with the name "Lucky Deal." When his career as an airshipman

was just beginning, he witnessed a disaster which was to
be a portent of calamities suffered by his own airships in
the future. Deal saw a hydrogen-filled airship diving
steeply toward the ground. He knew that it was out of
control and assumed that the men would just get a good
shaking-up, because the dive wasn't fast enough to kill
them. The ship disappeared from sight and seconds later
there was a brilliant flash, followed by a loud roar. The
airship had hit high-tension wires which ignited the hydrogen. Eleven men saved themselves by jumping, but
the other thirty-three crewmen died.

Deal's first fortunate escape from disaster came after
he had been chosen as rudder man for a flight of the
dirigible *Shenandoah*. The airship was going to fly over
St. Louis and Ralph Joffray, who came from that city,
begged Deal to let him go instead so he could see his old
hometown. Deal said okay, and Joffray died when the
Shenandoah was torn apart by a storm in 1925. The control car tore loose from the dirigible, carrying Joffray and
seven others to their deaths in an Ohio cornfield. Five
years later Deal married Joffray's widow.

Deal's last close disaster in a dirigible was in 1933
when another violent storm brought the *Akron* down into
the icy Atlantic Ocean. The seventy-six crewman didn't
have life preservers and only three survived. "Lucky"
Deal clung to a fuel tank until he was rescued by the
crew of a German oil tanker.

Hanging on a cable in a plane's airstream

Although Cowart survived a great ordeal under the
slow-moving dirigible, it takes much greater exertion to
fall out of an airplane, grab a cable, and hang on in the
brutal airstream until the plane is landed. Yet, this is
what James Tobin had to face in 1980.

Tobin, a civil service airman employed in the army,
was piloting a twin-engine, propeller-driven, cargo
carrier, when he saw a warning flash red on the instru-

ment panel. The light indicated an unlocked cargo door.
So Tobin went back to check while the copilot took
over.

As Tobin tinkered with the door it suddenly flew open
and he was sucked out into the sky. In a flash his left
hand grabbed a nylon cable on the airplane's exit and
entrance steps, which are attached to the cargo door and
which fold down when it opens. Tobin was not wearing a
parachute. His body, held to the plane only by his one-
handed grip on the cable, was shaken violently by the
220 mph wind created by the plane's speed. The plane
was nine thousand feet above the ground, and the temperature at that altitude was fifteen degrees Fahrenheit.
Tobin felt a strange sense of detachment. His mind was
working furiously, and it seemed to be floating somewhere free of his body.

The copilot, hearing a noise, looked back and saw
one of Tobin's feet dancing up and down outside the
open cargo door. Tobin felt the wind pressure decreasing
as the horrified copilot cut the plane's speed in half, and
with tremendous exertion he managed to swing his feet
against the side of the fuselage. Inch by inch he moved
his feet along the plane until he finally hooked his left
foot in the corner of the door jamb. Now, hanging upside
down, with his left hand on the cable and his left foot in
the door, he had a little better hold. But how long could
he hang on, with the airstream still equivalent to a hurricane force wind? He couldn't get his right leg hooked in
the door and his right arm was swinging free and flapping against his back.

The copilot couldn't hope to pull Tobin back into the
plane—Tobin was six foot two and weighed two hundred
pounds, and the Beechcraft U-21 plane, lacking an autopi-
lot, would soon go out of control without someone at the
helm. The copilot had no choice but to land as soon as
possible. He picked an airport which would allow a
straight-in approach, fearing that a turn would throw Tobin
from the plane.

The plane was dropping a thousand feet every minute,

and whenever the copilot looked back he saw Tobin still hanging on. The upside-down Tobin had a terrible shock when the copilot lowered the landing gear; he was looking up at the bottom of the wheels! He thought, "My head's going to hit first!"

He couldn't pull his body up, so he cocked his head at the sharpest angle he could possibly manage, and when the wheels touched the runway his head cleared. His punishment had not ended, however. The wheels shot pebbles into his face and a rock struck him squarely in one of his eyes. When the plane stopped rolling and Tobin tried to get down by himself, he couldn't let go of the cable.

Tobin survived to fly again, but first he had to recover from his battering. He had a broken arm, a black eye, torn cartilage in his rib cage, and lacerations around the hands and face from flying rocks. He felt completely changed by his experience.

"Little things I used to take for granted I don't anymore. Just getting up in the morning or watching one of the boys hook a fish is an unbelievable thrill.

"I never felt this way before, and it's wonderful."

CHAPTER 5

Crashing Into Mountains

The worst air route—with dangers primarily from nature rather than from antiaircraft weapons—regularly flown by aircrews was the "hump." Thousands of American transport crewmen flew supplies over the Himalayas from India to beleaguered China during World War II. The flights were essential because the Burma Road into southern China was in Japanese hands, but the loss of transport crewmen was horrendous—eight hundred and fifty airmen were killed before it was all over. During a single day in 1944, nine transports crashed in the Himalayas.

Eric Severeid, the former CBS television news anchorman, described the strain of hump flying:

"Hardly a day passed that the operations radio did not hear the distress signal of a crew going down in the jungle valleys or among the forbidding peaks. Few at that time were ever found again, and there was a saying among the pilots that they could plot their course to China by the line of smoking wrecks on the hillsides. It is not often that one sees fear in the faces of fliers, but I saw it here. Each one reckoned that it was only a matter of time before his turn would come; they had the feeling of men who know they have been condemned."

On his flight over the hump, Severeid had to bail out of his crippled plane, reaching safety only after living for a month with headhunters.

Why was the hump so dangerous? The flight across the peaks—ranging up to four miles above sea level and often hidden in clouds or covered by storms—was too great a challenge for the aircraft of the time. Most of the heavily loaded planes were brought down by a buildup of ice. Ice can choke engines, encrust and cut the power of propellers, coat and tear off antennas, turn windows opaque, and cover wings and tail, making an airplane unmanageable.

One of the most extraordinary adventures experienced by hump pilots was caused by icing. Pilot C. J. Rosbert, his copilot, Charles "Ridge" Hammel, and their Chinese radio operator took off from India in thick fog, climbed through torrents of monsoon rains, and found themselves flying through a blizzard of snowflakes at twelve thousand feet. They couldn't see their wingtips, but they felt confident. No Japanese fighter pilot would find them under these conditions, and in a short time the three fliers would clear the hump and begin their descent into China. But soon Rosbert saw a thin layer of ice beginning to cover the windshield and the wings. As the ice layer thickened, the plane began to drop slowly but inexorably. The pilots lost all visibility outside the plane as the windows became frozen over from the inside. Rosbert pressed the palm of one hand against the window until he felt the skin stick and then switched palms. Just before both hands had become numb, he melted a little two inch hole. He saw that they were passing through a cloud, and just as they emerged from the mist he saw a jagged peak directly ahead.

"Look out!" Rosbert yelled. "There's a mountain." He swung the ship into a violent bank as he kept his eye fixed to the tiny opening. The plane narrowly missed the cliff, but Rosbert watched with horror as something huge and dark came into view. He heard a shrill screeching noise beneath him, and the engines began to roar violently. His ankle was stabbed with pain that shot through his left leg. Then just as suddenly everything was eerily silent and stopped still.

"What happened?" Hammel, the copilot, asked.

"We hit a mountain," Rosbert replied. "What a crazy conversation," Rosbert thought. "Things like this don't happen. You hit a mountain at 180 miles an hour and that's that."

But the two pilots were alive, although Rosbert's ankle was broken and Hammel's ankle was sprained. They soon discovered that the radio operator was dead. They had come within fifty feet of smashing into the peak that Rosbert had first seen. Their steep bank away from the peak had paralleled the slope angle of the mountain, so that when they hit, the plane simply slid along the face of the cliff. A rock outcrop had caught the left engine, forcing them to a stop. If it had not been for that one outcrop, they would have smashed into another peak fifty feet ahead. The cabin was intact except for the crushed radio station. Both engines had torn off, thus preventing any fire.

The two pilots had been almost impossibly lucky, but they were going to need a tremendous amount of additional luck to reach safety. Their plane was tilted crazily, sixteen thousand feet up, against a Himalayan peak. Rosbert's broken ankle and Hammel's badly sprained ankle made it seem impossible that they could walk to safety, and they estimated that their emergency rations would last for only about a week. After spending the night in the plane, they found that it was covered by two feet of newly fallen snow. With the plane invisible to any searching fliers, they would have to try to escape on their own, covering hundreds of miles over some of the steepest topography in the Himalayas.

They figured that in five days their ankles would improve enough to move "without blacking out every few steps" from excruciating pain. They saw the edge of the timber line, five thousand feet lower and five miles away, and guessed that they would find a stream further down the mountain. A stream might lead to a river, and a river might run beside a house or village. But how could they possibly climb down such a distance of steep slopes with their smashed ankles and without any mountain climbing equipment? They would have to reach timber line before dark, because they could not live through the night in the ferocious cold of the unprotected slope.

On the third day after the crash they tried climbing down to timber line. However their injured ankles made movement so difficult that they only struggled downslope for two hundred yards before stopping. They barely made it back to the shelter of the plane by dark. The next day they tore their parachutes into strips to bandage their ankles and pried braces off the sides of the cabin to make splints. They set the splints and wrapped yards of parachute silk around them until their injured legs were fairly stiff. Then they wrapped more parachute material around their hands and feet for protection against the cold.

After trying to make sleds by prying up boards used to reinforce the plane's floor, they discovered that they could slide downslope even better by lying on their backs or sides and sliding ten, twenty, or fifty yards at a time. Finally, within sight of timber line, they came to a slope that was about five hundred feet straight down. Horribly scared, but without any choice in the matter, they went over in a cloud of snow, and landed with a crunch in a snowbank below, within earshot of running water.

After spending the night in a cave, they hobbled painfully over jungle-covered hills along the river for the next three days until the peaks became too steep to climb. Then they struggled down the river until they were stopped by a series of steep waterfalls. They found a vine hanging from the side of a cliff. The vine was a lifesaver because they were able to pull themeslves to the top, where notched saplings marked a trail.

The pilots had run out of food on the eighth day after their crash, and the next day they searched desperately for something to eat. Finally on the tenth day Rosbert fished a piece of fruit from the river that looked and smelled like a mango. He tried it, and soon learned that it wasn't a mango.

"The taste was incredibly vile; it seemed as if someone had struck me a blow in the mouth. I retched horribly and rolled on the ground in agony. Ridge Hammel had to try a bite, too, and he went through the same torture. But there is some good in everything. Our stomachs were numb for the next three days. Even starving as we were, we could not bear the thought of food."

After thirteen days, they came to a fork in the river. One way led westward toward Burma and their base in India, and the other route led eastward into the wild mountain country of Tibet. If they had been thinking clearly they would have taken the westward branch, toward their base, but they were so exhausted that they merely followed in the direction they were facing, toward the east. This proved to be another lucky break because they shortly came to a hut which contained inhabitants of this very remote region.

These native Himalayan people proved to be cheerful, hospitable, and very curious about their new guests. Rosbert and Hammel were apparently in a place where white men had never been seen. Rosbert reported that:

"They had to feel our clothes, try out our shoes, run the zippers up and down the front of our flying jackets amid roars of gleeful laughter, blink their eyes in childlike amazement when we let them turn on our flashlight, listen with ever widening eyes to the ticking of our watches."

Rosbert and Hammel were still a long way from reaching civilization. After more than two weeks with the natives, the two pilots met a Tibetan trader who had seen white men. His son carried a note from the two Americans to a British scouting column, about four days march away. Finally, after about 23 days with the natives, Rosbert and Hammel were overjoyed to see a British medical officer walk up to them. He told them that because of the war, the British column had only recently come into this region where white men had never ventured. If the British had not been even as close as four days away the fliers might never have been found. It was another great piece of luck.

It took sixteen more days of hiking, with the natives carrying the injured men over some of the roughest terrain, to get out of the mountains. The two Americans reached their base forty-seven days after crashing into the mountain. They were tremendously glad to be back, but at the same time they couldn't help feeling regretful at leaving their new friends:

"We both confessed to a heavy tug at leaving these strange people who had been so kind and so hospitable to a couple of strangers who, dropping suddenly out of another world, had been taken into their family and treated as brothers these many days."

Hammel was ready to fly a month after returning to the base, but Rosbert was sent home to a Seattle specialist to have his ankle remade. Rosbert found that, "The doctor could not understand how, with one broken ankle and one badly sprained, we had lived through the hundreds of miles we walked. He called it a miracle."

Crashing into the Andes

Almost three decades later, in 1972, there was another quite unbelievable mountain airplane crash—this time high in the Andes of South America. Members of the Old Christian Brothers Boys' School rugby team of Montevideo, Uruguay, and their fans and relatives were flying on a Uruguayan Air Force F–27 turboprop plane toward Chile. The pilot miscalculated and began to let down for a landing while still in the middle of the mountains. When the plane dropped below the clouds the boys saw that one wing tip was only about ten feet from a mountain. "Is it normal to fly so close?" one boy asked another. "I don't think so," his companion replied. Just then the right wing tip hit the side of the peak and the entire wing broke off, somersaulted over the fuselage, and cut off the tail. The navigator and steward, who had been playing cards in the plane's tail section, and three boys still strapped in their seats fell out of the gaping hole in the tail to their deaths. Moments later the crippled plane's left wing broke away, and the blade of the propeller slashed into the side of the fuselage before falling away into space.

The remaining forty people on the plane were in about as bad a situation as anyone could be. They were in an uncontrollable, wingless, tailless plane, its momentum carrying it toward the mountain at 230 mph. The plane landed on its belly in a steep valley and slid like a toboggan on the sloping surface of steep snow. Two more boys were sucked out the back to their deaths, but the fuselage held together during its dash down the snowfield. As the skidding plane slid to an abrupt stop some seats broke loose from their mountings and hurled their occupants forward, causing injuries which were to prove fatal to another eleven passengers.

The survivors had been incredibly lucky to get down alive, but, as in the case of Rosbert and Hammel, they still faced nearly insurmountable odds. They had crashed at 11,500 feet on October 13, 1972 (early spring in the southern hemisphere), and the Andes were to have very heavy snowfalls that year. The plane's radio wouldn't work after the crash and the top of the plane was white, so there was little chance of being spotted from the air. Planes searching for the missing aircraft could see no trace of it. The heavy snowfalls made the rugged terrain impassable. If the battered Uruguayans didn't freeze to death, they would almost certainly starve.

As the twenty-seven survivors lay in the fuselage trying to face their perilous dilemma another disaster struck—an avalanche crashed into the plane. Those who had escaped burial as the snow rushed into the plane dug frantically to free others engulfed in the white mass. Eight of the passengers were suffocated by the avalanche, leaving a total of nineteen survivors.

The Uruguayans spent seventy days on the mountain. During this living nightmare three more died, reducing their number to sixteen. Finally as the snow began to thaw, two of the boys, Roberto Canessa and Fernando Parrado, managed to hike down the mountains into Chile, walking fifty or sixty miles over a period of ten days.

The search for the missing group had long since been abandoned. The fact that sixteen of the group were not only alive but in most cases remarkably healthy, seemed truly incredible to their friends and relatives. Then the truth came out—they had survived by eating parts of their dead companions! They told their stories to author Piers Paul Read, who turned the experiences into a best seller: *Alive: The Story of the Andes Survivors* (J.B. Lippincott Co., Philadelphia, 1974).

After they had gone through their ordeal, the survivors learned how close they had been to safety all along. If they had followed a valley leading from the tail end of their plane, they could have reached a road in three days. Five miles to the east was a hotel, which although open only in the summer, was stocked with food.

Why humans are sometimes tougher than airplanes

The two mountain plane crashes that we have reviewed had survivors because the planes hit slopes at precisely the most favorable angles (helped in the Andes by the slope being snow-covered), resulting in the fuselage being substantially intact after the crashes. However, four passengers survived the crash of Japanese Airlines Boeing 747 in 1985, even though the plane flew directly into a mountain and was shattered into widely scattered debris. The plane, which became uncontrollable after large parts of its tail broke away in flight, plunged into a pine covered, steeply angled ridge. Enveloped in fire as the impact ripped apart the fuel tanks, it smashed through trees, uprooting them as they tore the plane apart. Many fragments of the plane, as well as the passengers, were flung into ravines and gullies on either side of the narrow ridge.

Rescue searchers flying over the desolate, fiery scene concluded that no one could possibly have survived the crash. Not even a helicopter could safely land on the forty-five degree slope in the night darkness, so the searchers set up camp forty-two miles away from the crash site.

When the first men reached the crash site, fourteen hours after the accident, they were astonished to see someone moving. Yumi Ochiai, twenty-six, an off-duty Japanese Airlines flight attendant traveling as a passenger, was lying between airline seats, seriously hurt, with a broken pelvis and arm fractures, but conscious. Next the rescuers found Keiko Kawakani, twelve, in a tree and unhurt except for cuts and torn muscles. The third and fourth survivors, Hiroko Yoshizaki, thirty-four, and her daughter Mikoko, eight, were found under debris. Both had broken bones.

Five hundred and twenty people had died, but a physician concluded that others would have survived if help had come ten hours earlier. How could anyone survive such a horrendous impact? All were seated near the tail, supposedly a relatively safe location in a crash, and Yumi Ochiai recalled seats and cushions tumbling down on her as the plane crashed. These may have cushioned her from much of the violence of the impact. Another important factor in their survival undoubtedly is that the human body can survive impact forces which will demolish virtually any airplane.

Let's compare the human body's resistance to very rapid deceleration with that of an airplane. Crop-dusting aircraft, which are very prone to crashing into power lines, telephone poles, etc., are built to withstand strong crash forces. They have reinforced cockpit structures, with a welded tubing "birdcage" above the pilot to shield him in case of a turnover. Such a cockpit can withstand crash forces as high as forty-five Gs (one G is equal in value to the acceleration of gravity). As mentioned in Chapter Three, Cornell University scientists calculated that a man who fell 150 feet from a smokestack survived 162 Gs when his body hit the ground. He recovered from his injuries quite rapidly. A race car driver, David Purley, survived 180 Gs when his car decelerated from 108 miles per hour to zero in twenty-six inches in a crash at the Silverstone circuit, Northamptonshire, England, on July 13, 1977. Some fall survivors have undoubtedly recovered from even higher G forces. If crash victims are not smashed by debris from a disintegrating aircraft and if they escape the effects of fire, amazing crash survivals are indeed possible!

Motor vehicle crashes over cliffs

Aircrews and their passengers aren't the only ones to survive crashes against steep slopes. Let's talk about some hairbreadth escapes where vehicles careened off roads and plunged over cliffs.

In the mid-1950s a motorist told of a horrifying experience:

"I was driving down a one-lane canyon road when suddenly I met a truck coming head-on toward me. Involuntarily, I jerked the steering wheel to the right. My car plunged over the edge of the road and down into the canyon. I felt I was going to die.

"I suppose everything happened in a few seconds, but it seemed that I had all the time in the world, and I wasn't the least bit concerned about dying. My affairs were in good order, and my wife would get my insurance.

"Then I saw that my car was crashing head-on toward a canyon rock. So, I thought, this was the way that fate had picked for me to die. The impact against the rock would drive the steering wheel shaft back through my body. I felt very little emotion about my approaching death. In fact, I was like a third person looking on. My body would be killed, and I would stand by and watch; a curious onlooker.

"It occurred to me then that I could escape from death if I moved out from behind the steering wheel, pulled up my knees to protect my body, and put my arms and elbows across my face.

"Should I do this? I debated the question, and I decided that I'd rather not. Better to die outright, I decided, than to be crippled for life. Better to die quickly now, than die later from a lingering disease.

"I agreed with this viewpoint so thoroughly that, when the car was caught by the top of a pine tree and deflected from the rock, I was more annoyed than elated.

"I escaped with a broken arm and some cuts and bruises. My friends say it was a miracle. If so, it wasn't one of my choosing, because given a choice between life and death, I had chosen death."

Another near disaster after a vehicle roared over a cliff occurred when a bus carrying a team of seven Japanese acrobats went over the edge near Tokyo in 1933. The bus careened violently down the mountainside, overturning several times, and the team seemed headed for oblivion. A few hundred feet down, however, the bus's plunge was slowed for a fraction of a second when it rolled over a large rock. During that instant, the seven trained and agile acrobats hurled themselves through open windows and landed in the branches of a tree. The acrobats were shocked and bruised, but alive.

Mountain crash in spacecraft

Our last mountain crash story will relate the horrendous flight of an out-of-control Russian spacecraft. The Russian cosmonauts Vasiliy Lazarev and Oleg Makarov blasted off on April 5, 1975, for what was supposed to be a two-month space flight. When they had reached an altitude of ninety miles and a speed of about ten thousand miles per hour, their rocket's third stage and its spent second stage didn't separate properly, and the spacecraft began to tumble violently.

The cosmonauts radioed their control center about the emergency, but at first nobody believed them. Data received at the control center showed that the engines were normal, and the tumbling rate was so high that it was off the scale, leading controllers at the Moscow Mission Control Center to the conclusion that the control center reading was defective. Violent, earthy curses from Lazarev finally convinced the ground specialists that the cosmonauts were in big trouble. The spacecraft was blasted loose from the aberrant rocket by a command from the ground, and it began a steep plunge back to earth.

The cosmonauts knew that their flight path took them near China, and they were worried that since they were now off course they might land in that unfriendly country (two Russian helicopter pilots, who had mistakenly landed near this area earlier, were captured by a Chinese patrol and had languished for three years in a Peking prison).

"Are we going to land in China?" the cosmonauts asked the ground controllers. "We have a treaty with China, don't we?"

The cosmonauts greatest problem, however, was reaching the ground still alive. Normally, returning spaceships decelerate slowly along a lengthy near-horizontal path, but this spacecraft was dropping at such a steep angle that their chances looked very poor. The G forces, which soon exceeded the normal reentry level of four Gs, kept increasing until they reached reentry forces never encountered by a returning space capsule. They surpassed eight Gs, the emergency level; they surpassed fifteen Gs, the design level of the spacecraft; and finally the G meter went completely off the scale, somewhere over eighteen Gs.

When the forces of deceleration began to slacken, the cosmonauts were still alive, but they were hurtling straight down toward the Altai Mountains, where any rescue attempt would be hindered by the fact that the sun had just set and darkness was approaching.

A series of parachutes opened, slowing the capsule's fall, and the Russians landed gently on a snow-covered slope. Then one final, terrible danger appeared as they began to roll in their capsule downslope toward a precipice. Just before they reached the edge of the precipice, the parachute lines snagged on some scrub pines. Their wild ride was over, fifteen minutes after they had left the launch pad two thousand miles to the west.

The cosmonauts came down near a village, and their parachute had been spotted in the twilight sky. A rescue party reached the capsule within an hour and the cosmonauts were delighted to hear them speaking Russian rather than Chinese—the spaceship had come down on the safe side of the border.

The injured cosmonauts spent considerable time recovering from their injuries. Makarov flew on another space mission in 1978, but Lazarev was assigned to a new role at the cosmonaut training center.

CHAPTER 6

How to Crash with Flair

*J*ohn MacGavock Grider, an American pilot who was killed in World War I, described in his diary a day spent watching first World War aviators learn to fly.

"Cal and I went down to Stamford [The location of the base] to spend the day and nearly died laughing. Our stomachs are still sore."

The commanding officer of the training base told the cadets that they were needed in the war and that they were all going to solo that afternoon. "They nearly fainted. Some of them had less than two hours of air work and none of them had more than five.

"The first one to take off was a bit uneasy and an instructor had to taxi out for him. He ran all the way across the field—and it was a big one—and then pulled the stick right back into his stomach. The six [DH-6, a type of airplane] went straight up nose first and stalled and hung on its propeller. Then it did a tail slide right back into the ground.

"The next one did better. He got off and zigzagged a bit, but instead of making a circuit he kept straight on. His instructor remarked he would probably land in Scotland, because he didn't know how to turn.

"Another one got off fairly well and came around for his landing. He leveled off and made a beautiful landing—a hundred feet in the air. He pancaked beautifully and shoved his wheels up through the lower wings. But the plane had a four-bladed prop on it, and it broke off even all around. So the pupil was able to taxi on into the hangar as both wheels had come up to the same distance. He was very much pleased with himself and cut off the engine and took off his goggles and stood up and started to jump down to the ground, which he thought was about five feet below him. Then he looked down and saw the ground right under his seat. He certainly was shocked.

"Another took off fine, but he had never been taught to land and he was a bit uncertain about the operation. He had the general idea all right, but he forgot to cut off his motor. He did a continuous series of dives and zooms. A couple of instructors sang a dirge for him:

'The young aviator lay dying, and as 'neath the wreckage he lay
To the AK Emmas around him assembled, these last parting words did he say:
"Take the cylinder out of my kidney, the connecting rod out of my brain,
From the small of my back take the camshaft, and assemble the engine again.'

"There were a lot more verses, but I can't remember them. We thought sure he was gone, but he got out all right and made a fairly decent landing, but not where he had expected.

"The next one didn't know much about landing either. He came in too fast and didn't make the slightest attempt to level off. The result was a tremendous bounce that sent him up a hundred feet. He used his head and put his motor on and went around again. He did that eight times and finally smashed the undercarriage so that next time he couldn't bounce. Then he turned over on his back. The CO congratulated him and told him he would probably make a good observer.

"They finally all got off and not a one of them got killed. I don't see why not though. Only one of them got hurt, and that was when one landed on top of the other. The one in the bottom plane got a broken arm. I got quite a thrill out of that."

Why were no trainees killed in all these crashes? In addition to being very lucky, they undoubtedly survived because the DH-6 training planes were so slow: their top speed was only sixty-six miles per hour! The number of crashes survived by some early pilots in their sluggish, treacherous planes was incredible.

Survivor of fifty plane crashes

Louis Bleriot, the French aviator who became the first pilot to fly an airplane across the English Channel, survived fifty crashes. An awed British journalist announced that:

"Monsieur Bleriot is the most daring aviator in the world. He has learned how to save himself when he falls, and when spectators rush up, expecting to find that he has broken a leg or an arm, he picks himself up and begins to give directions to his mechanics as to the necessary repairs. He seems to realize in an instant the exact extent of the damage and to know exactly what must be done to make the machine airworthy."

Bleriot explained his ability to survive crashes in this way:

"A man who keeps his head in an aeroplane accident is not likely to come to much harm. What he must do is to think only of himself, and not of his machine; he must not try to save both. I always throw myself upon one of the wings of my machine when there is a mishap (as the plane crashes), and although this breaks the wing, it causes me to alight safely."

Bleriot continued his amazing string of luck until December 1909, when he finally had one accident too many. While making an exhibition flight over Constantinople (now Istanbul), he crashed onto a rooftop and broke both wings and several of his own ribs. Sobered by this accident, he gave up flying and devoted his efforts to the manufacture of airplanes.

Why did Bleriot's planes crash so often? The monoplane design which carried him across the English Channel was one of the most advanced airplanes of its day, but compared to modern planes, it was an extremely dangerous aircraft. The late Frank Tallman, a very courageous and skilled movie stunt pilot, described its shortcomings:

"It's hard to put in words readily explainable to the modern pilot how perfectly awful it really is to fly the Bleriot and what a great admiration I have for the pilots whose raw courage often outstripped their piloting knowledge. Of the 120-odd flying hours I have spent in Bleriots, I am sure no five minutes have gone by without adding a deepening color tone to the streak down my back. My first attempted flight in a Bleriot ended ignominiously in a ground loop when the mighty airflow of a two-cylinder Aeronca engine wasn't sufficient to lift the tail—or, in fact, to control the rudder at all! This same airplane, later powered by a sixty-five horsepower Continental, came within an ace of wiping out a portion of the U.S. Air Force's new (at that time) F-102 Convair interceptors. The Bleriot broke ground nicely for the Air Force show; then, at an altitude of about a hundred feet, the realization suddenly came to one very startled pilot that full deflection of the control wheel apparently had no effect on the wing warp (warping of the wings by cables was used for turns— a function performed by ailerons on more modern airplanes), and with a very sick feeling I slanted in toward the line of parked interceptors, out of control. By skidding the rudder and dropping the nose, I managed, at the last possible second, to ditch in a parking area without damage except to my shattered nerves.

"In spite of a slow actual ground speed (about forty-four to forty-eight mph), there is still no experience in my years of flying to equal the sick feeling you have when a wing goes down in gusty air and you head for the ground unable to pick up the wing in spite of full opposite control."

Strange light plane crashes

Modern light planes, just like the light, slow planes of the pioneer pilots, are responsible for some very surprising mishaps—crashing in all sorts of locations. On February 11, 1986, a student pilot, Dean Plath, fifty-eight, and instructor pilot Ed Washburn, sixty-seven, were making a practice instrument night landing approach to Southern California's Ontario International Airport when they flew into 220,000-volt power lines about three miles from the airport. After striking the two one-and-a-quarter inch cables, eighty-five feet above the ground, the Cessna 172 flipped upside down, slid for five hundred feet along the wires to an unsteady stop, and then hung belly-up by its propeller and front landing gear. Power to the high voltage lines was automatically cut on impact, but the area suffered no blackout because the power was automatically switched to another circuit. The student pilot later reported that, "At first, I thought we were on the ground. I tried to get out of the airplane. I released the safety belt, opened the door, and using the shoulder harness, I lowered myself down to the wing." The instructor pilot then shouted, 'We're in the wires, not on the ground. For God's sake, come back in.' "

Rescuers used a crane to support the plane, while firefighters rode a hydraulically operated ladder up to the plane. The operation was difficult because rescuers had to stabilize the forty-five-hundred-pound plane, so the two men could be brought out without unbalancing it and causing it to fall. The men were finally brought safely to the ground, four hours after crashing into the wires. The rescue was watched live on television by millions of Southern Californians and one television station assignment editor said that, "We got literally thousands of calls ... people were saying how wonderful it was—'better than a movie.' "

In 1937, Ernst Udet, a top German World War I ace and a great stunt pilot after the war, unintentionally demonstrated another way to survive a collision with a wire. Udet flew a fighter plane smack into a thirty-thousand volt trolley wire. The impact jerked the car violently uphill, but the wire slowed Udet's plane in the same way that naval aircraft are slowed by an aircraft carrier's arresting cable. Udet stepped from the crashed fighter plane without a scratch.

In favorable circumstances light planes can survive a landing in a tree. Hans Rudel, a German dive bomber pilot who was shot down thirty times and wounded five times during World War II, included a landing in a tree among his many near fatalities. Rudel and another Luftwaffe officer named Fridolin flew a Fiesler Storch (a light, slow plane) to their air command headquarters, which was located in a castle surrounded by tall trees. They managed to land in a small clearing, but their takeoff—Rudel by then was flying with one leg amputated and another in a cast—was a near disaster. Rudel described the experience (here translated somewhat awkwardly from his book, *Stuka Pilot*):

"We take off again toward the tall trees on a gentle rise. The Storch is slow in gathering speed; to help her start I lower the flaps a short distance before the edge of the forest. But this only brings me just below the tops of the trees. I give the stick a pull, but we have not sufficient impetus. To pull any more is useless, the aircraft becomes nose heavy. I already hear a crash and a clatter. Now I have finally smashed my stump if nothing worse. Then everything is quiet as a mouse. Am I on the ground? No, I am sitting in the cockpit, and there, too, is Fridolin. We are jammed in a forking branch at the top of a lofty tree, rocking to and fro. The whole tree sways back and forth with us several times, our impact was evidently a bit too violent. I am afraid the Storch will now play us another trick and finish by tipping the cockpit over backwards. Fridolin has come forward and asks in some alarm, 'What is happening?'

"I call out to him, 'Don't budge or you will topple what remains of the Storch off the tree into a thirty-foot drop.'

"The tail is broken off as well as large pieces of the wing planes; they are all lying on the ground. I still have the stick in my hand, my stump is uninjured. One must have luck on one's side. We cannot get down from the tree, it is very high and has a thick, smooth trunk. We wait, and after a time the general arrives on the scene; he has heard the crash and now sees us perched up aloft on the tree. He is mighty glad we got off so lightly. As there is no other possible way of getting us down, he sends for the local brigade. They help us down with a long extending ladder."

In 1942 Wallace D. Smith of Louisville, Kentucky, was flying a plane at low altitude when he spotted a girl he thought he knew. He waved at her and was delighted to see her wave back. Distracted, he flew the plane into a tree top, an electric wire, and finally another tree top, where the plane came to rest. Smith climbed down the tree and rushed to the girl to assure her that he wasn't hurt. She wasn't the girl he had thought, but a total stranger.

Crashing in severed tail sections

After having discussed survivals of slow aircraft crashes, how about some crashes that were much harder to survive: those in which people crashed in detached parts of aircraft.

William Stannard had the unusual experience of riding to the ground in the separated tail of a Royal Air Force bomber in 1943. Stannard was a radio operator and gunner in a Ventura bomber that, accompanied by ten other bombers, was on its way to bomb the Amsterdam power station in daylight. Near the Dutch coast, German fighters caught the lumbering bombers and began to riddle them with their cannons. One of the bombers had already been hit near the coast and it turned for home—the only one of the eleven British planes to survive. The fighters then shot the other ten bombers out of the sky one after another.

Stannard's bomber was one of the first to be fatally hit.

Stannard was spread-eagled on the floor at the rear of the bomber; his job was to fire two machine guns through a turret in the floor to protect the bomber from attacks from below. Cannon shells came crashing through the plane, killing the upper turret gunner. Stannard looked toward the nose of the plane to see if the other two crewmen aboard the bomber had survived the attack, but all he saw was a torrent of fire that filled the fuselage. He had another horrible shock when he realized that his parachute, which was stowed in a rack by the main door, was directly in the middle of the fire.

The navigator leaped out of the escape hatch in the cockpit roof, holding a loose parachute pack in his hands. (He managed to clip the pack on in midair during his fall and he landed safely.) The draft from the opened cockpit hatch sucked the flames away from the main door and Stannard rushed forward, eagerly grabbing the scorched but still usable parachute pack. Just before he could clip the pack on and jump out the door, the flames surged back, and he had to retreat to the rear of the fuselage. As he stumbled backward, the silken canopy spilled out of the pack onto the floor. Before he could gather up the folds, a blast of searing heat forced him into the narrow opening in the tail. With his chute now lost forever in the fire, Stannard squeezed his body as far back into the tail as possible. He could only hope that his end would come quickly as he saw the blast furnace–like fire begin to melt the fuselage metal and turn it into molten rivulets only a few feet ahead of him.

Stannard was almost within the grasp of the flames when he heard an explosion and saw the entire blazing forward part of the bomber tear away from the tail section and fall slowly below him, mercifully carrying the fire away with it.

The fuselage had broken off just ahead of where Stannard's two machine guns were attached to the floor, about ten feet from the tip of the tail. He saw the guns bouncing gently up and down on their elastic suspension lines that

ran up to the top of the fuselage. Looking out past the
guns, he saw a clear blue sky, and nine thousand feet
below him was the coast of Holland. He could see that he
was slowly revolving—one moment he would see the hori-
zon of the North Sea, then a blurry view of land, then the
sea again. The rotation was slow and gentle and not at all
uncomfortable to him. The tail surface had a certain
amount of lift and the twin fins and rudders also added
stability. Therefore, instead of plunging down, the tail unit
spiraled down like an autumn leaf.

Stannard sat in his short piece of fuselage with his back
against one wall and his feet against the other. After the
horror and scorching heat of the fire, he relished the cool,
gentle breeze which blew past him. During the three or
four minutes that he spent in the spiraling tail, he said that
he felt calm and unafraid. He attributed this to the enormous sense of relief that he felt after escaping the fire. He
much preferred to die by falling in the tail unit, and his
feelings of deliverance overshadowed any feelings about
the new form of death he faced.

During his fall, Stannard was upset not by his own approaching end, but by thoughts of the shock it would give
to his mother. "I thought a great deal of my mother," he
said, "and I was the apple of her eye. I was her only surviving son and there was an exceptionally strong bond between us. She was the only person I thought about as I
came down, and I thought about very little else."

At first Stannard had felt as though he was descending
very slowly, but as he neared the ground, he could see that
he was falling rapidly. Sooner than he expected, the tail hit
the top of a tall pine tree, tilted slightly, and began to rip
down through the tree. After the tail hit the tree, Stannard
wedged himself tightly between the walls, expecting to be
thrown out. The first impact in the thin, springy branches
at the top of the tree was gentle. As the tail dropped to the
ground, larger branches snapped and splintered, and the
crashing sounds were fearsomely amplified in Stannard's
metal shell. But the tail didn't turn over as it passed
through the tree and he rode it safely to the lowest

branches. As the tail dropped gently onto the ground it finally turned over, tipped Stannard out, and the elastic straps wrapped around his throat in a choking grip. For a moment he was too dazed to free himself, but he managed to force the straps apart and pull his head out.

Stannard staggered away from the tail, semidelirious and obsessed with the idea that the other crew members had come down with him. He began to frantically search for them, stumbling around the lawn of a beautifully kept garden and shouting their names.

The tail had landed in the garden of the very wealthy Miss Willink van Bennebroek. Her astonished gardener saw the tail tear apart the first tree in the garden and drop onto the lawn. The gardener's amazement increased even more when he saw a man crawl out of the tail and begin to run around the lawn shouting at the top of his voice.

The gardener took Stannard into an enormous manor house where the regal-looking Willink van Bennebroek offered him a glass of red wine. She sent for her doctor to treat his injuries, which were astonishingly minor. Before the tail broke off the aircraft, he had received a burned forehead and left hand, and two flesh wounds from exploding ammunition. His fall had caused only a slight concussion and a cut on the head. Unfortunately the friendly visit didn't last long, as a member of the Gestapo came to take him away for two years captivity in a prisoner of war camp. After the war, Stannard returned to Holland to thank once again Miss van Bennebroek and her doctor and gardener.

Stannard's fall of nine thousand feet in a tail unit, while extraordinary, is not unique. Vesna Vulovic, a hostess for Jugoslavenski Aerotransport (JAT), fell thirty-three thousand feet inside a section of the tail unit when a DC-9 blew up over Czechoslovakia on January 26, 1972. She suffered terrible injuries in contrast to Stannard's minor ones. She had a fractured spine and legs and suffered a broken arm. She was in a coma for three days, and after she regained consciousness she remained in the hospital for an additional six months.

Rescuers found her lying partly on the ground and partly in a small compartment of the airplane. stream. She recovered completely and went back to work for JAT, although not as a stewardess. She remembered nothing of her fall.

"All I can recall is stepping onto the plane to start the flight. From then on it's a complete blank until my first memories of waking up in the hospital."

Toward the end of World War II, an American tail gunner rode 13,500 feet to earth in the severed tail section of his B-17. The bomber was sliced in two by a collision with another B-17 over Belgium and only one crewman successfully bailed out from the main section of the bomber—all the other crewmen in the forward part of the airplane were killed. In the tail Joe Frank Jones, Jr., a nineteen-year-old gunner, couldn't get out through the jammed escape hatch or through a very small window by the tail turret. He was trapped in the falling tail unit.

After the tail crashed to earth, Belgian peasants found Jones lying in a field still alive and took him to a hospital. There he remained unconscious for eight days while doctors treated him for relatively minor injuries. He had a lacerated tongue, a ruptured blood vessel in his stomach, and a bruised thigh. When Jones regained consciousness he was asked what he had done when he realized that he could not escape from the falling tail. Jones replied that he had unbuckled his parachute, sat down, lit a cigarette, and waited.

While in a German prison camp, Nick Alkemade, whose three-and-a-half-mile fall without a parachute was described in Chapter Two, shared a hut with another prisoner who had been the rear gunner of a British flying boat. The flying boat was shot up over Norway, and an explosion had blown the plane's tail turret completely off—with the rear gunner still inside it. The turret and its gunner fell into a deep snow drift, where several hours later some Norwegians found him nearly frozen, but still alive.

Fliers trapped in aircraft fires

It would be an oversight to finish this chapter about crashes without including some accounts of extraordinary escapes from aircraft fires, which are often a much greater threat to aircrash victims than the impact force itself. We saw earlier how William Stannard was saved when his bomber's tail unit broke away from the blazing forward part of the plane, but crewmen in burning World War II aircraft generally had a far greater chance of escape than did the German crewmen of World War I Zeppelins when their hydrogen-filled airships caught fire far above the earth.

The bombing raids of England by Zeppelins brought terror to many Englishmen, but more Zeppelin crewmen were killed than Britons. A greater proportion of the Zeppelin crews who served in the Naval Airship Division met death (about forty percent) than that of any other branch of the German Navy—more even, according to some figures, than the percentage of losses in the submarine service. Seventeen airships were lost with all hands, and in sixteen of those cases the ship's destruction resulted from a hydrogen fire. The airships were forced to fly as high as possible to escape destruction from British fighter planes. When the hydrogen-filled Zeppelins caught fire at these great heights, there was virtually no chance to get down alive in the slowly descending airships. Parachutes were issued to Zeppelin crewmen for a few months early in 1917, but they were withdrawn because of the great need to save weight. The crews had no faith in the primitive chutes and no parachute jumps were ever made from a Zeppelin during the war. Essentially the only choices were to burn with the airship or jump to a less painful death.

A Zeppelin crewman, Machinist's Mate Heinrich Ellerkamm, recalled a unique nighttime escape from a burning airship high above England:

"I thought we were over the sea on our way home [they were at an elevation of about 13,700 feet]. It was time to check the fuel supply for my motor—I had pumped petrol

up to the gravity tanks above the gondola some hours before—and I told my helper to take over. There was a faint
light of dawn in the east, and as I climbed the ladder,
suspended in space halfway between the gondola and the
hull, I heard a machine gun firing. There below us, dim in
the light of dawn, was the English flier. I stepped onto the
lateral gangway inside the hull; we were below pressure
height and I could look aft. There was another burst of
gunfire, and I could actually see flaming phosphorous bullets tearing through the after cells. I watched with a horrified fascination. This I knew must be the end! Any one of
those bullets could set our hydrogen on fire. There was an
explosion—not loud but a dull *woof*! as when you light a
gas stove. A burst of flame. Then another explosion. One
gas cell after another was catching fire over my head. My
first thought was not to be crushed under the wreckage in
case we were over land, so I climbed further up among the
girders. Flames were dancing everywhere, and the heat
was overpowering. My fur collar caught fire; I tried to beat
it out with my hands. The weight of the big two-engine
gondola aft was dragging down the stern, the ship tipped
vertically and down we plunged, a monstrous roaring ban-
ner of flame hundreds of meters above my head, and the
wind whistling through the bared framework. I noticed the
draft was driving the flames away from me, but it was only
a temporary respite. I thought of jumping and remembered
Korvettenkapitan Schutze, when he was our commander,
saying, 'Better to smash against the earth and perish at
once than to burn to death trapped in blazing wreckage on
the ground.' No, it isn't true that we carried poison or
pistols to shoot ourselves when the ship caught fire. Hand-
guns were forbidden.

"I was still arguing with myself when a light appeared
below—whether on land or sea I could not tell. Suddenly
there was a terrible, continuous roaring-smashing of metal
as the stern struck the ground and the hull structure collapsed beneath me. I found myself on the ground with the
breath half knocked out of me, the framework crashing
down on top of me, fuel and oil tanks bursting on impact

and their burning contents flowing toward me through the shattered wreckage. I was trapped in a tangle of red-hot girders, the heat roasting me alive through my heavy flying coat. If I had lost consciousness I would have burned to death. But I could still think and move. With all of my strength I forced some girders apart—I never felt the pain of my burned hands until later—and burst out of my prison. I fell full length on cool, wet grass. In front of me, frightened horses were galloping away across the field, their tails in the air. I heard the roar of an engine, and saw a British plane circling low over the wreckage, the pilot waving to me. Already it was almost full daylight.

"The fire was roaring at my back. Staggering to my feet, I turned back to the wreck. Korvettenkapitan Schutze had jumped as he always said he would; he was dead, his legs buried up to the knees in the ground.

"English civilians helped me to drag Lieutenant zur See Mieth, still alive, out of the radio cabin in the control car. One of them later took me to his home, where I collapsed unconscious. Later I asked to be taken to see Mieth, but it was forbidden.

"I can't explain how I survived. All I can say is that my gondola was one hundred meters from the tail cone, and the tail structure broke the force of my fall, while the bow did not collapse on me entirely."

The escape described by Ellerkamm was the only one in the eight-year history of the German Naval Airship Division where crewmen survived a ride to earth with two million cubic feet of blazing hydrogen. Ellerkamm escaped with only minor burns. Mieth survived with two broken legs, and a third man was so badly injured that he died of his injuries on Armistice Day, 1918. Fourteen other crewmen died in the fire or jumped to their deaths.

How does it feel to be completely engulfed in the flames of an aircraft fire? One graphic account was given by Bill Simpson is his book, *One of Our Pilots is Safe*. Simpson crash-landed his burning bomber in the Ardennes during World War II. The aircraft exploded before he could release his straps and the flames poured over him.

"My hands were searching frantically for the release clip holding my straps together. Great sheets of searing flames rushed between my legs and up to thirty feet above me. In that first rush of heat my hands were burned and they seized up solid. They were completely useless. I was trapped by my straps and could not move. The awful realization that I was about to be burned to death took possession of my mind. A tremendous white heat enveloped me. I could feel my flesh burning, but the pain I felt was mostly mental.

"I let my hands drop onto my knees and curled myself up, waiting for the release of death. My whole mind was full of a bloodcurdling scream: but no sound came. Behind my head the electric klaxon screamed out its strident note, reminding me to lower my wheels before making a landing.

"As I sat there waiting to die, my mind raced back over the years. I saw a kaleidoscope of scattered, ever-changing scenes. Some were happy, some sad—the most vivid moments of my life. Afterward, I was surprised to find that on the point of death life is lived in vivid retrospect, the mind grasping for the last time at the memories which had stimulated it in life. But I did not die."

Simpson was dragged clear by his gunner and observer and rolled in the wet grass. Although horribly burned, he later recovered both his health and appearance, helped by new techniques in plastic surgery.

CHAPTER 7

A Funny Thing Happened on the Way Down

Some chuteless air crewmen during World War II tried to ride down with a buddy who had a parachute. The ideal way to have done this—where the crewmen had parachute packs that snapped onto harnesses over their chests— would have been for the men to stand side by side and for each to attach one of the two rings of the pack onto one of the snap hooks on his harness. Since the parachute was designed to take a strain of more than a ton during opening, both men could probably have reached the ground safely. The big problem was that most aircraft escape hatches, often on the floor or top, were too small for two men to squeeze through together. In these cases the "passenger" usually had to ride on the parachutist's back. In the few cases where such dual bailouts were attempted, the shock of the opening parachute was so great (it has been compared to the shock experienced in violently braking a car traveling at one-hundred miles per hour) that the passenger's desperate grip generally wasn't strong enough, and he was thrown off to his death.

However, one such passenger had such a strong grip that he managed to hang on through the opening of the parachute. In 1943, the rear gunner of a British bomber lost his parachute in a fire and had to leave the plane on the back of the wounded radio operator. They bailed out at around fifteen thousand feet, the parachute jerked open, and still the gunner stayed on the parachutist's back. It took about ten minutes to reach the ground and several times during the descent the radio operator's injuries caused him to pass out briefly. Each time he revived, he felt the gunner still on his back. Finally, a few hundred feet above the ground, the radio operator blacked out again, and when he regained consciousness he was shocked to find that the gunner was gone. Soon afterward, the radio operator hit the ground and lost consciousness. The Germans who found him told him that the gunner's body was only a few feet away. If they had jumped just a thousand feet lower, they would have reached the ground safely before the gunner's exhausted arms lost their grip.

Stories about lives saved by parachutes can be found in great abundance in the files of the Caterpillar Club of the Irving Air Chute Company. Those who escaped death by using an Irving chute sent in application forms to the company detailing their adventure. If the account was deemed true, they were admitted to the club. Ian Mackersey read through thirty thousand files and also interviewed many survivors for his fascinating book *Into the Silk* (published in 1958 but unfortunately now out of print). By 1958 over eighty thousand lives had been saved by Irving chutes. Among the incidents listed in the Irving company files is a hard-to-believe story about two men who were saved by one parachute in an incredible incident over Germany on the night of June 11, 1944.

Chuteless fliers who fell onto other parachutists

Two Australians were blown out of a bomber—one wearing a parachute and one without one—seventeen thousand feet over Germany in 1944. After a drop of twelve thousand feet (to five thousand feet above the ground) the man with the parachute pulled his ripcord. Just as the chute first began to open, the second man collided with him and grabbed his legs, and both floated safely to earth together. This is how it happened:

Joe Herman, the pilot of the bomber, was very jittery as they flew through searchlight beams and flak bursts on their way to the target, and for the first time in thirty-three missions he told his crew, including gunner John "Irish" Vivash, to clip on their parachutes. Herman, however, was too preoccupied with the run to the target to have his own parachute brought to him from its rack in a compartment behind him.

After the plane had dropped its bombs and headed back toward England, Herman felt a frightening thud behind him. He swung the plane violently to the left in an attempt to escape the flak, but he felt two more heavy thuds from behind and knew that they had been hit again. The first thud had been a direct hit in the fuselage and the second and third bursts were in the wings; the fuel tanks were set afire on both sides and the wings were burning from root to tip.

Herman ordered the crew to bail out, but Vivash, the gunner, replied that his leg was injured and asked for help getting out. Herman undid his seat harness and went back for his parachute and to help Vivash. He saw Vivash crawling along the fuselage toward him dragging his injured leg, but before helping him, Herman decided to collect his own parachute off its rack. As he was about to reach for the chute, he saw the right wing fold back in a great sheet of flame.

The bomber snapped over on its back and before Herman could grasp his parachute the plane began to spin and he was thrown against the side of the fuselage. He raised both hands up to brace himself, and at that moment the bomber exploded.

When Herman found himself falling through the cold night sky in a shower of debris and without a parachute, he panicked and began to struggle violently in the air because he so desperately wanted to do something to save himself. After a few seconds he relaxed his body as he resigned himself to the appalling inevitability of his fall.

Herman saw several moonlit pieces of debris falling near him and with a flicker of hope he began to look for his parachute among them. His hopes were soon dashed when he saw nothing resembling a parachute case. He had another glimmer of hope, when he saw the silvery ribbon of a river below. He knew the water could smash him like dry land if he hit it, but he still mightily hoped that he might be saved by landing in it.

Herman had little sensation of falling even though he was slowly tumbling head over heels, with alternating glimpses of stars and the ground. He felt as though he was being gently swung around on a feather bed, and because there was no discomfort, at times he felt a sense of detachment, as though he were merely a witness rather than a victim. These feelings, however, were generally overwhelmed by the terror he felt when he thought of the final crunch. He knew that he would feel nothing when he hit, but thinking about it and waiting for the end sent chills of horror through him and gave him an overwhelming urge to scream.

Suddenly he crashed into something with a resounding smack and thought, "This is it." But he found himself still alive and hanging onto something with both arms. Then, in midair, five thousand feet above the ground, Herman heard a voice he recognized. It was the voice of John Vivash, asking, "Is there anybody around?" Herman was grasping Vivash's legs and there was a fully opened parachute floating over them. Herman replied, "Yes I'm down here." Vivash asked, "Where? Where are you?" And Herman answered, "Here just below. I'm hanging onto your legs." (Both of Vivash's legs had been hit by shrapnel, so they were too numb to feel Herman hanging there).

Just when Herman's aching arms felt like they were about to slip off, the two men floated down on into a small clearing in a pine forest and crashed to earth. Vivash landed on Herman's chest, breaking two of the pilot's ribs. Herman was bruised from head to foot, and his face and ears and left leg were all badly cut, but these injuries seemed minor in comparison to the all but certain death he had faced only moments before. After Herman bandaged Vivash's legs with strips of parachute silk, the two Australians managed to evade the Germans for four days before being captured.

During the days before their capture, the two airmen analyzed the chain of events that led to their midair meeting.

When the bomber had exploded both men were blown out, but while Herman had been fully conscious during his fall, Vivash blacked out in the explosion and didn't revive until after he had fallen for a long distance. They had undoubtedly been falling only a few yards from one another, and one of the dim objects which Herman had seen close by in the moonlight was most likely the unconscious Vivash.

When Vivash had partly regained consciousness he pulled the ripcord (he did not even remember this act later). As his chute began to pull out of its pack, Vivash swung out under it like a pendulum so that his legs were extended nearly horizontally at the end of the swing. This is normal at the moment of opening. Herman, who was tumbling slowly head over heels, must have bumped into Vivash's legs when Herman was face down and also horizontal. At this moment Vivash's chute, which was just starting to open, had only begun to slow him and he was still traveling very fast. Therefore Herman and Vivash were still traveling at roughly similar speeds and Herman was able to hang on. A second or two later, Vivash's opening parachute canopy would have slowed him from 120 mph to 11 mph, and if Herman, falling at 120 mph, had crashed into Vivash, floating down at 11 mph, Herman would have bounced right off.

Both Herman and Vivash returned to Australia after the war. Herman became a civilian pilot and again demonstrated his aptitude for amazing good luck by crawling unhurt out of a crash in 1954 which demolished his plane. Vivash was killed a few years after the war in a motorcycle accident.

You might think that an escape as improbable as Joe Herman's would be unique, but a World War I balloon observer named William S. Lewis had a very similar experience.

Lewis and Lieutenant Higman went up to five thousand feet over no-man's-land at Vimy Ridge in France to locate a German artillery piece which had been persistently lobbing shells at the Allied trenches. Unknown to the two British balloonists, a fault in a valve had prevented hydrogen from escaping as the gas expanded on its way up. Without warning the balloon burst and then slowly collapsed into the basket. Lewis and Higman struggled out from under the collapsing envelope and jumped out of the basket.

Higman's parachute opened and he began to float safely down, but Lewis's chute wrapped itself around the balloon's support cable. Lewis struggled to shake himself free from the falling balloon cable. His chute finally tore loose, but the canopy ripped in half and Lewis began to fall very fast with a narrow stream of silk flapping violently above him.

Lewis had seen the ghastly outcomes of several parachute accidents, and falling horror-stricken toward the ground he closed his eyes. He felt himself land on something soft, opened his eyes, and saw that he was on top of Higman's parachute. They were about three thousand feet above the ground.

At first it appeared that Lewis's unlikely landing would cause the death of both men. Higman's parachute canopy collapsed and Lewis found himself lying on the folds above Higman, desperately gripping a handful of rigging lines. As they began to drop rapidly to earth Lewis apologized, "Sorry, I couldn't help it." Higman replied, "It's all right, old man, but couldn't you find some other bloody patch to fall on? Millions of bloody acres about you, yet you pick on me!" As he watched the ground rushing up toward them, Higman added, "It looks like the finish."

Lewis was about to reply when the canopy reopened with a loud "pop." As it billowed out, Lewis slid off and, still holding onto the rigging lines, he dangled between the canopy and Higman. As they neared the ground Lewis's grip began to weaken and he slid down the lines until his feet were below Higman's. Lewis landed heavily but safely among Canadian support trenches with Higman rolling on top of him.

A variation on falling onto a chute was the case of a British paratrooper with an unopened chute who was saved by a parachute being used to drop a container filled with guns and ammunition.

Sgt. Tom Spencer was making a training jump from a C-47 near Haifa (now a part of Israel) in 1943. He jumped a few seconds after the container and its chute were thrown out of the plane at four hundred feet. Spencer had no ripcord to pull: a static line opened each parachute automatically as the paratroopers fell from the plane. Spencer's chute didn't open, however, and he faced the appalling prospect of smashing into the ground in about five seconds.

In the next instant Spencer fell feet first into the rigging lines of the container parachute. The container chute with its cylindrical cargo container had been swinging back and forth like a pendulum about fifty feet below Spencer when he left the plane. Luckily it swung out under him at the moment that he reached it.

Spencer was, ill-advisedly, wearing shorts, and he felt fierce stabs of pain as the rigging lines bit into the flesh of his legs. The chute crumbled and folded up on the side where Spencer had landed and he began to drop at a dangerous speed.

Spencer's legs were tangled in the lines and held him in a position that would cause him to land on the base of his spine if he couldn't struggle free. He wriggled loose at the last moment and, holding onto the rigging lines above him, drew himself up as high in the lines as possible.

The container clanged onto the ground and Spencer landed very hard beside it. Spencer had fractures of the spine, leg, and pelvis, and he had leg burns from his impact in the rigging lines. But he recovered quickly, and four months later he was able to walk normally again.

Bailing out too low for chute to open properly

Another type of near fatality survived by some very fortunate parachutists occurs when the bailouts are extremely close to the ground. While modern ejection seats allow safe bailouts even from a plane sitting on the ground, the airmen of World War II (before the time of ejection seats) had to jump out and allow one or two seconds to pass before they pulled the ripcord—otherwise the chute could foul on part of the plane.

The lowest height to bail out of a World War II airplane in level flight was generally thought to be around three hundred to four hundred feet above the ground. But there were some extraordinary parachute escapes from much lower altitudes.

Lt. Earl W. Knier, an American fighter pilot flying over Normandy, strafed a German antiaircraft battery and, in return, got shells through his motor and left wing. The plane burst into flames and his clothing caught on fire in the burning cockpit. He was too low to bailout, but he couldn't stay in the airplane. So he jumped out of the burning airplane. When a body leaves a speeding airplane it initially travels at about the same speed as the plane, and Knier's plane was doing 350 miles an hour when he left it. With his hands across his knees he was streaking along at a tremendous speed just above the ground. He didn't think it would do any good but he pulled his parachute ripcord. The great speed of his body quickly opened the canopy and pulled the silken pod along through the air behind him before he had fallen more than a small distance toward the ground. He didn't know for sure how far he was above the ground, but he thought it must have been less than one hundred feet, because when he started to drop, there was just enough height for him to straighten out and hang perpendicularly from the chute. He just swung in an arc and hit the ground, rolling. He extinguished his burning clothing, ducked into a hedgerow, and drew his revolver. He saw a soldier running toward him and feared that the man might be a German. He heard with relief a midwestern voice say, "You flyin' boys is always in a hurry, but I bet you couldn't do that again."

Flight Lt. Dudley Davis of the Royal Air Force had a similar parachute escape in 1940 from a burning bomber which he estimated to be fifty feet above a German harbor. He had skimmed along fifty feet over the water at Wilhelmshaven harbor to drop a mine under the keel of the German battleship *Tirpitz*. Hit by antiaircraft fire, Davis stayed on his course, dropped the mine beside the battleship, and zoomed over the ship's superstructure with flames streaming behind his plane.

Davis hoped to escape by flying low over the water through the outer harbor, but the controls became ineffective and the searing heat in the cockpit forced him out onto the right wing. Hanging onto the cockpit edge, he knew he was too low to bail out, but the plane was about to stall and it started rolling to the right.

Davis pulled the ripcord. The parachute streamed back in the airstream, the canopy filled, and Davis was yanked off the wing. His back bounced off part of the aircraft, and a second later he hit something hard. He found himself lying on his side on a breakwater stone that projected out into the sea. His descent, like Knier's, had been a pendulumlike swing directly onto his landing spot.

Another way that men who bailed out "too low" were saved, was in having their unopened parachute canopies snatched by trees just before their bodies hit the ground. Flight Lt. C. A. R. Crews, his navigator, and his gunner were on their way to attack a bridge when German antiaircraft fire set their bomber on fire. Skimming low over rolling wooded country, they couldn't crash land. They knew they would have to bail out, but the engine had lost power, and Crews could only coax the plane up to two hundred or three hundred feet above the trees.

The flames gushed at the British crewmen and gave them no choice but to crawl out on the wing and jump. As Crews fell he saw the green tree tops rush up at him and he shut his eyes. About two seconds later he hit the trees. His face burned where the pine needles scraped the skin, and then he felt a tremendous jolt. He opened his eyes and found himself hanging six feet off the ground on rigging lines held in the top of a pine tree by the half-opened canopy. He saw the gunner hanging from an adjacent pine tree in precisely the same way. Both men dropped to the ground, cut and bruised, but otherwise uninjured. Between the two trees that saved them lay the body of the navigator. His parachute, like theirs, had streamed but had no time to open. The navigator had plummeted down where there was no tree to catch him, and he was killed instantly.

One fortunate flyer was saved when his unopened chute was grabbed by a tree, and with the assistance of other shrubbery. Flying Officer Ken Wright, an RAF fighter pilot, was diving toward his airfield when the tail of his plane broke off. The crippled aircraft spiraled toward the earth until the wings ripped off about three hundred feet above the ground and the figure of the pilot was seen to hurtle out. A speck of white appeared behind him as the chute began to open, but before more than a few feet of silk had emerged he crashed through an oak tree and hit the ground.

An ambulance drove to the spot to collect the pilot's body, but although the men saw torn parachute fragments in the tree, there was no body below it. A few yards from the tree they saw a freshly punched hole in a hedge, and beyond the hedge in a grainfield there was a trail of flattened oats. At the end of the trail lay Ken Wright, alive and in amazingly sound condition. He had a fractured breast bone, a few other chipped bones, lots of bruises, and a concussion. Within seven weeks he was flying a fighter again.

With the help of several witnesses, Wright's escape was pieced together. Wright had no ejection seat, but when the wings broke off, the seat, which was attached to the top of the wing center section, was hurled out of the plane. The safety straps which held Wright in the seat had snapped, releasing him. Wright was unconscious at the time of his ejection and the cable from the ripcord handle to his parachute pack had apparently caught on the flap lever and been torn off. This opened his chute pack at the same moment that he was thrown out of the cockpit.

As Wright tore through the oak tree, the small amount of the canopy which had emerged from his parachute pack snagged in the branches, quickly pulling out the rest of his canopy and the rigging lines then tore off, leaving Wright to finish his journey with only his parachute harness left but at a drastically reduced speed. If his emerging chute had not caught in the tree he would certainly have been killed.

CHAPTER 8

Extraordinary Exits in the Air

In the following accounts it is apparent that not all explosions are disastrous to close-by humans. Some, in fact, are lifesavers.

Sgt. Roger Peacock, a gunner in a RAF bomber, was spared to live another day by an explosion after bailing out too low in 1940. After Peacock's bomber was hit by flak while returning from a night raid over Germany, both engines stopped. The pilot gave the order to bail out and, assuming that Peacock had already jumped, both he and the observer left the plane.

But Peacock did not hear the order and stayed in the aircraft. He began to worry as the plane kept spiraling toward the ground. He asked over the interphone, "Shall I bail out now?" There was no answer, so Peacock repeated the question. Still hearing no reply, he assumed that the pilot was too busy for conversation and decided not to bother him for a while.

Finally Peacock couldn't stand waiting any longer. He rushed forward to the cockpit, saw that he was the only one left in the plane, and jumped out.

As Peacock fell, he saw through the darkness that the ground was much too close. Just as his parachute had begun to stream, the bomber crashed beneath him and exploded. A blinding flash lit up the countryside, and as he was about to fall into the blazing wreckage a sudden blast of hot air snapped his parachute canopy completely open and carried him upward and sideways away from the burning aircraft. A few moments later Peacock landed safely in a field some distance away from the wreckage. Five minutes later he saw the pilot, who had jumped from the spiraling aircraft six thousand feet above, float to earth nearby.

An explosion saved another Briton, Lt. Comdr. P. E. I. Bailey, at low altitude in a very different way. Bailey was flying a fighter over the Normandy beaches in 1944 when his plane was misidentified as German and fired upon by a British ship. The plane, its tail shot off, began an out-of-control dive toward the beach. The cockpit hood had been damaged so that he couldn't jettison it. As the ground rushed up toward his diving plane, trapped and feeling that he would die in an instant, Bailey had a feeling of great calm, and thought how serenely beautiful was the scene below.

Two hundred fifty feet above the beach, and still trapped in the cockpit, Bailey pulled his ripcord in a last hopeless, futile act. Just as he yanked the cord, he heard a tremendous bang, felt a jolt as his chute opened, and almost immediately found himself lying on the beach. The external fuel drop tank on Bailey's plane, nearly emptied by the flight from England and mostly filled with vapors, had exploded, tearing the plane apart and blowing Bailey out to safety.

Now let's look at an incident in which an explosion not only blew a flier out of an airplane but also blew open his parachute, allowing him to make an unconscious descent to the ground, where he revived much later. Group Capt. C. T. Weir was piloting a British bomber in 1944. When he reached the target—an aqueduct—and heard the bombardier call, "bombs gone," he was aware of a great white flash and a roaring noise in his ears. A one thousand pound bomb dropped by another British bomber, flying above, had landed directly on Weir's aircraft.

Three hours later, about midnight, he regained consciousness lying in the mud of a canal a short distance from what remained of the aqueduct. He had a broken jaw and a gash in each leg, and his chute was spread out beside him.

Weir was shivering and noticed that he was sopping wet. He soon figured out the reason. He had landed in the canal before the following planes blasted apart the aqueduct. He floated there unconscious until the bombs broke the aqueduct and allowed the water to rush away, leaving him on the mud like a stranded fish.

As Weir's eyes became accustomed to the darkness, he saw that the canal bottom, its bank, and the surrounding fields were pockmarked with hundreds of bomb craters. He had lain unaware in the middle of the area that one hundred British bombers had saturated with one thousand pound bombs.

Weir saw two bombers burning in a nearby field. One was his bomber, and the other was one that had been flying directly behind his. The second bomber was brought down by the same explosion that destroyed Weir's aircraft. Weir had been blasted out of his seat, up through the cockpit roof. The explosion had blown open his parachute, and he flew away in a shower of debris. He was the only one of fourteen men in the two bombers to survive the blast. Like many others who survived apparently certain death with parachutes, he lived to see peacetime, having escaped the dangers of further combat in a POW camp where so many fliers spent their remaining wartime service.

Fliers trapped in spinning, crashing bombers

Another peril for World War II fliers was the centrifugal force of a stricken, spinning plane, which could pin them against the plane's interior, making their movement to escape hatches impossible. Often it was incorrectly assumed that the men were "rooted to the spot by fear," too panic-stricken to move.

The pilot of an American bomber described what these men experienced. When his plane began to spin he tried to jump through the open doors of the right forward bomb bay:

"Instead of falling out of the right forward bomb bay, I landed in the left forward bomb bay, the door of which had not opened. It felt as if some invisible force was pressing me against that door, and I found it very difficult to move my arms or legs. Only by tremendous exertion was I able to grasp the edge of this catwalk. The ship gave a sudden lurch and I was catapulted out of the bomb bay. My parachute opened immediately, and as my body was swinging to a position directly beneath it, I hit the ground. It's my opinion that the effect of the centrifugal force was not strong enough to hinder my escape until the ship had made one complete turn. After that, except for reaching out with my hand, it was impossible to move."

In another case, a gunner pinned to the floor by centrifugal force and unable to drag himself to a hatch shoved his parachute out the hatch and pulled the ripcord. He managed to hang on to the straps as he was forcibly dragged out of the plane by the opening parachute. He survived and suffered only cuts and bruises.

Crashing to earth in a stalled, spinning aircraft from a great height is almost invariably fatal, but at least one airman did survive such a crash. Sgt. A. Stephen described his experience in a British Halifax bomber that spun to the ground after becoming coated with ice during a bombing raid on Hamburg.

"All at once, the whole aircraft started shuddering, and the back of my turret was blotted out with ice. I turned the turret round and, just for a few seconds, I could see the wings covered with ice and the props sailing round like white windmills. Then my view was blotted out again.

"The aircraft was losing flying speed and I felt it stall. I got out of the turret quickly to get my chute, for I felt we were not going to get out of this, and I was no sooner inside the fuselage when we went into a spin. The G force [centrifugal force] was very strong; I could not even lift my arm. I was in the center section at this time and I felt someone kicking to get to the exit, but he was pinned down like me. The spin seemed to go on for hours but, then, there was a crash and everything was thrown about.

"When I came round, the thing I was most aware of was the silence, and I felt very tired and fell asleep, as I thought. I suppose I passed out. When I came round the second time it was daylight, and I saw that I was sitting in a heap of wreckage and Bert, the engineer, was lying beside me. I could not move but I heard someone talking outside and gave a shout. They were German soldiers and they came and lifted Bert and me out of the remains of the Halifax. I remember cursing them for lifting me by the legs because they were fractured. The soldiers put us down in a field about a hundred yards from the wreckage and I saw the part I had been in was just the two wings and center section. The target indicators were hanging out and the petrol tanks were right above them. How the lot did not blow up, I'll never know.

"Bert was moaning pretty bad and I held his head off the ground. He gave up, finally, and died in my arms. We had drunk quite a lot of beer together, Bert and I, but no more for him and not for me either in the near future. I learned later that the rest of my crew had been killed in the crash, which did not surprise me as the wreckage was scattered across three fields."

Parachutes snagged on crashing planes

Some parachute escapes have been thwarted when opening parachute canopies snagged on parts of an aircraft. For example, Lt. Zivota Boskovic, a pilot in the Yugoslav Air Force, bailed out of a fighter at two thousand feet after it broke up during an aerobatics demonstration in 1938. He began to float down in a shower of debris, but almost immediately the fuselage, minus wings and tail, spun down onto the parachute. The canopy collapsed and the silk wound itself around the fuselage. For a thousand feet Boskovic, dangling on his shroud lines, was spun like a ball on a string round and round the falling fuselage. Then, about a thousand feet above the ground, the canopy tore from top to bottom, the chute fell away from the fuselage, the split canopy opened out again, and Boskovic floated to earth. He landed—according to the imperfect English on his application form to the Caterpillar Club—"unhurtedly on very hard ground." Boskovic concluded his application by stating that as a result "of this dreadful event, the confidence to the Irving parachute increased still."

In 1941 an uncontrollable RAF aircraft over Somerset had a civilian passenger who decided to bail out. Unfortunately his ripcord handle caught on part of the aircraft, and the chute opened before he could get clear of the plane. The canopy wrapped itself around the tail, and he was dragged along behind the airplane on his shroud lines. The pilot, who had also planned to jump out of the careening plane, saw the passenger's predicament and decided to try and land. The plane crashed and blew up, yet both men escaped. The pilot was thrown clear and the dangling passenger released himself from the chute harness just before the plane hit the ground. He fell a few feet to the ground, rolled along, and came to a stop with only a broken leg and minor head injuries. He sent an application to the Caterpillar Club, but he was turned down because the parachute had in no way checked his fall.

Supersonic ejection

The problems that World War II airmen had in jumping from disabled aircraft were in large part overcome by the development of ejection seats. Fliers could now escape from the deadly iron grip of centrifugal force, and they could safely get away through the fierce rush of air created by high-speed jet aircraft. However, ejections at supersonic speeds were another matter.

In 1955 George Smith, a civilian test pilot, experienced the strongest blast of wind survived by a human being, when he ejected from his out-of-control jet fighter at sixty-five hundred feet as it dove toward the ocean at supersonic speed.

Smith was immediately knocked unconscious by the supersonic airstream, but his parachute opened automatically. He floated down with about a third of his parachute canopy torn away. His clothes were in ribbons and his shoes, socks, helmet, and oxygen mask all had been carried away by the wind. He was bleeding from cuts on his forehead, chin, and feet.

He landed very close to a fishing boat, and just after he hit the water a puff of breeze inflated his parachute canopy. This, plus a small amount of air trapped in what was left of his clothes, kept his face out of water, until the boat could reach him. His life jacket, which had to be inflated manually, was limp and useless since he hadn't regained consciousness.

When he was first taken to the hospital, Smith had a barely noticeable pulse and his blood pressure was so low that it was not registering. However, in a few days he was out of extreme danger and began a gradual recovery that would keep him in the hospital for six months.

Smith had suffered tremendous G forces as the supersonic wind blast slammed into his body. His blood became, in effect, many times heavier than normal as it sloshed back and forth. This caused many hemorrhages throughout his body. Smith had blood in both middle ears, and his face was badly swollen and colored a dark purple by bleeding under the skin.

The G forces caused Smith's eyeballs to strain against his eyelids as their natural tendency to continue on in the direction that they were moving pulled at their root and produced tremendous pressures on the retina. For many days he couldn't see as a result of hemorrhaging in the eyeball and damage to the retina. The whites of his eyes had become solid red from subconjunctival hemorrhages. Smith's lips, ears, and eyelids were badly bruised and bleeding from fluttering at incredible speed in the supersonic windstream. Air had rammed into his mouth and down his throat, causing his stomach to inflate like a balloon.

Before his parachute opened, Smith tumbled wildly in space. Flailing of his legs had caused dislocation and sprain of his hip joints. His lower intestine was damaged by the violent gyrations and required surgery. The violent swinging of Smith's arms shook off his wristwatch as well as his tight-fitting gloves and ring.

Eventually Smith was able to return to test flying. His most permanent injury was to his liver—he was forbidden the use of alcohol for the rest of his life. One thing Smith never did recover, however, was any memory of his supersonic bailout.

Col. John P. Stapp, who used himself as a human guinea pig on a rocket sled at Edwards Air Force Base, was able to supply what Smith couldn't—an account of what it felt like to be hit by the sort of G forces that would be encountered in a supersonic bailout. In 1954 Stapp—seated on a rocket sled with no windshield—was shot down the track and then, after the rocket finished burning, was stopped violently by water brakes. He was wearing a windproof helmet with a plexiglass visor and he had a bite block to protect his teeth. To prevent flailing of his arms and legs, he was tightly bound by straps. Eighty minutes were spent in making all the straps fast.

Colonel Stapp wrote his impressions of the experience:

"On entry into the water brakes, the face immediately felt congested with severe pain around the eyes, as though they were being pulled from the sockets. Vision became a shimmering salmon-colored field with no images. Evidently the pupils were impinged against the stretched upper eyelids and the visual sensation was caused by light coming through the lids. The congestion and pain increased noticeably during the exposure to more than twenty-five Gs for more than one second. Sensation in the eyes was somewhat like the extraction of a molar without an anaesthetic. This pain was sufficient to override sensations caused by impingement on harness straps even though later abrasions and contusions were visible at all strap pressure areas.

"When the sled stopped, the visual impression of shimmering salmon color not only persisted but was present when the eyes were forced open. There was a marked exophthalmos, which made it difficult to open the eyes without using the fingers. The chest strap was so tight that it was extremely difficult to breathe. Mental confusion, like that of struggling against the onset of anesthesia, was present. As soon as the chest strap was loosened and the bite block removed, normal respiration was possible and the confusion diminished. There was no loss of consciousness at any time."

To escape the terrible decelerative forces experienced by Smith and Stapp, some military aircraft have been equipped with escape capsules that can be ejected and parachuted to earth with the fliers safely enclosed in them.

CHAPTER 9

Happy Landings After All

D*o you* like practical jokes? Capt. Charles R. Sisto of American Airlines did. He played what was probably the most infamous practical joke in airline history on two fellow pilots.

In 1947 Sisto, Capt. Melvin Logan, and Capt. John Beck boarded an American Airlines DC-4 (a propeller-driven, four-engined aircraft) in Dallas for a flight to Los Angeles. Sisto was in command and Logan in the copilot's seat as the plane took off with forty-nine passengers. Beck, a DC-3 pilot who was becoming familiar with the DC-4, sat behind Sisto and Logan in a spare seat. The plane was rumbling along at its cruising altitude of eight thousand feet in sparkling clear skies when Sisto suggested that Beck take over the controls. Beck, eager to fly the DC-4, settled into the pilot's seat, and Captain Sisto moved back to the spare seat.

As the plane droned along, Sisto decided to play a joke on his friend. Sisto reached down and fastened the gust lock—a device used to lock the rudder, elevator, and ailerons while the plane is on the ground so the control surfaces will not flop around in the wind.

The plane began a steady climb. Puzzled, pilot Beck

adjusted trim tabs on the plane's control surfaces to bring the nose down. With forty-nine passengers in the rear, the plane stayed tail heavy with its nose up. Further adjustments still didn't bring the nose down and Beck said to Logan, "What's the matter? This plane wants to climb today."

Hearing that, Sisto testified later, "I decided that the joke had gone far enough. I disengaged the gust lock, and we went over like a shot out of a barrel, BANG."

With the controls moved to an extreme position to bring the nose down, the release of the gust lock caused the airliner to plunge down abruptly, first vertically and then beyond the vertical until the plane was actually upside down. Beck and Sisto did not have their seat belts fastened and they were both thrown to the top of the cockpit, where they accidentally struck three of the four propeller-feathering buttons. With three propellers feathered, the plane lost power and the dive slowed. This accident saved the lives of all on board, although the pilots didn't realize it at the time.

With the power cut, copilot Logan—the only one whose belt was fastened, keeping him in his seat—managed to roll the airliner from its upside-down position back to level flight only 350 feet above the ground. Sisto and Beck were still groggy, and Logan flew the plane to a safe landing at El Paso.

Thirty-five of the badly shaken passengers had minor injuries, but no one was badly enough hurt to require hospitalization, even though many had been thrown from their seats during the plane's violent half loop. A man from New York said, "I have been through eternity." An unfortunate young French student who had been in the lavatory was doused with the entire contents of the plane's chemical toilet. He was apologetically informed by the airline that, "This is not normal operating procedure in American airplanes."

At first, all three pilots told the investigating board that they thought the automatic pilot had failed. However, a tight-lipped, grim-faced Sisto finally confessed, and the airline accepted his resignation.

Diving airliners have terrified passengers on several other occasions. During the early years of jetliner flight, Pan American Capt. Waldo Lynch, following an old tradition, left the cockpit of his Boeing 707 and went back to visit the passengers. The copilot, in charge, thought that the automatic pilot was on, as is usual and almost necessary in flying the heavy jetliners. However, it wasn't. The copilot, busy talking on the radio, didn't notice at first that the plane had nosed over at thirty thousand feet and was going into a dive. The dive became so steep and the G forces so strong that pilot Lynch had to get down in the aisle and crawl on his hands and knees back to the cockpit. Together, the two pilots, using all their strength, managed to pull the plane out of its dive after a plunge of twenty-four thousand feet. The Boeing airliner's wings were bent, but it flew to a safe landing. From that time forward the Federal Aviation Administration forbade captains going back to visit with the passengers.

In November 1963 air turbulence caused a DC-8 to stall and dive at a sharp angle. An airliner diving steeply at high altitudes can reach supersonic speeds. Most airliners, including the DC-8, are not designed for such speeds and can go out of control and ultimately break up in the air. The plummeting DC-8 recovered from its supersonic dive only after the pilot put all four engines into reverse thrust—normally used to brake landings after the plane is on the ground—and one engine pod was torn completely off the wing in the process. The plane returned safely with its three remaining engines.

Even more horrifying out-of-control dives have been survived by military pilots. Chuck Yeager, while test flying the rocket powered X-1A in 1953, was told by engineers that the plane, because of its small tail, would probably lose stability if flown faster than Mach 2.3 (2.3 times the speed of sound). Yeager flew the plane to Mach 2.4, establishing a new speed record, and then learned that the engineers were correct. The plane flipped out of control and began to tumble wildly end-over-end, snapping, rolling, and spinning in all directions like a cork in ferocious river rapids.

Yeager, despite being strapped to his seat, was thrown violently around the cockpit. His head cracked the canopy and his flung-about body bent the control stick and smashed the inner lining of the plane's pressurized cockpit during a ten-mile fall which lasted about fifty seconds. Yeager was certain that he would be killed. However, the X-1A, which had no ejection seat, did not break up, and the dazed, battered, and admittedly terrified Yeager finally managed to get the uncontrollable, tumbling plane into a normal spin. He recovered from the spin and flew back to Edwards Air Force Base to conclude what was probably the wildest flight ever to end with a safe landing.

Hans Rudel, whose crash into a tree was described in Chapter Five, went into an unintended vertical dive while flying a German dive bomber during World War II and pulled out so low that he actually flew through forest trees. Rudel had banked violently to avoid collision with another German dive bomber while flying in a fierce thunderstorm and his bomb-laden plane plunged straight down into black clouds.

As Rudel desperately pulled back on the stick to restore the plane to level flight he heard a loud thump and thought, "There now, I am dead." But the plane was still flying, and as they emerged from the clouds Rudel and his gunner were astonished to see two great holes in the wings on either side with large birch limbs sticking through them. Rudel's plane must have recovered to level flight so near the ground that it swept along an avenue of birch trees, or between two birch trees, where the branches stuck in the wings. The sturdy Stuka dive bomber brought its crew safely back to their base, branches and all.

Brilliant forced landings

Some pilots have made unusual landings when their engines failed. In 1936 Wesley Smith was flying a DC-2 (the slightly smaller predecessor of the DC-3) to Chicago's Midway Airport when one of its two engines failed about seventy-five miles east of the city. He flew on but lost the second engine as he was making his final approach to the airport. By a fantastic bit of flying, he landed the plane in Chicago on a vacant corner lot without a scratch on any of his twelve passengers. However, because Smith had come down a half mile from the airport he was declared guilty of bad judgment in flying on with only one engine, and he was fired by the airline.

Bob Hoover, a great air show pilot whose routines include dazzling aerobatic displays in planes with feathered propellers, once found himself in a plane with a dead engine and insufficient altitude to return to the runway at Wright Patterson Air Force Base. Hoover, who has survived about twenty major accidents during his flying career, made it back by bouncing his wheels off a passing truck to give himself altitude to clear a chain link fence and reach the runway.

Scott Crossfield also belongs in the list of pilots who have made unique landings. Crossfield was given a chance to fly the XF-92-A while a test pilot at Edwards Air Force Base. The XF-92-A, an experimental prototype of the first delta-wing airplane, was considered by many pilots to be the worst-flying airplane built in modern times. It was badly underpowered, the controls were supersensitive (Chuck Yeager said that a pilot could get the plane to lift off the runway for its takeoff if "you just blow a little on the stick"), and the brakes were very weak.

For his first flight in the plane, Crossfield planned to taxi down a dry lake bed at high speed, lift off the surface briefly to get the feel of the plane, and then set it back down. He made his test run and plopped the fighter back onto the dry lake bed, but he could only slow it down slightly. It was barreling at frightening speed toward some sand dunes at the edge of the dry lake. Crossfield could see that he would not be able to stop in time, and he knew that if the fully fueled plane plowed into the dunes, it could explode into a fireball and incinerate him.

Crossfield's mind raced furiously as he thought of a way to save his life. He would allow the plane to roll on until just before it crashed into the dunes. Then he would retract the landing gear, turn on all the fire extinguishers, blow off the canopy, and as the plane skidded onto its belly into the sand dune, jump out and run like hell.

As he rolled inexorably on toward a fiery end, Crossfield noticed a narrow dirt road going off toward the left. He jammed on his left brake with all his might and it seized for a split second, then fell off onto the dry lake bed, a molten mass. However, the plane began to turn slightly to the left, and when it reached the edge of the dunes it went streaking up the road with its tires blowing out and burning. There was a danger that the jolting ride could snap off the nose gear, leading to a smash-up, but the plane stayed straight and level and finally ground to a stop about a hundred yards up the road.

It was a tradition at Edwards Air Force Base to name paved roads after test pilots killed in action. After the wild ride on the dirt road it was facetiously called the "Crossfield Pike." Another test pilot told Crossfield, "You know, Scotty, you're the only pilot still alive at Edwards who has a road named after him."

Some pilots have made extraordinary landings after vital parts of their aircraft suffered structural damage. On a DC-3 training flight with no passengers aboard, a student pilot stalled the aircraft and sent it into a spin. The instructor, Capt. William Joseph Hull, wrenched the plane out of the spin, but the strain tore off both wing tips and took the ailerons with them. Because ailerons are used to turn and bank an aircraft, Hull was in the same fix as a driver in a speeding automobile whose steering column had just snapped. In a stupendous display of airmanship, Hull managed to fly the plane back to a safe landing by manipulating his engine throttles, thereby using differences in power between the two engines to turn the plane.

A balloon explosion and no parachute

One of the most dismal structural failures for a balloonist is to have a balloon explode. John Wise, a pioneer balloonist, described what happened after his hydrogen-filled balloon became "fearfully expanded" at an elevation of thirteen thousand feet. He was flying over Pennsylvania in the wake of a passing thunderstorm in 1838.

"At this critical moment I became somewhat excited; and as I looked over the side of my car [the balloon's gondola], I observed the sparkling coruscations of lightning springing from cloud to cloud a mile beneath me. I took out my watch, noted on my log book the time—twenty minutes past two. As I was about to return it to my pocket, thinking at the time whether it were not best to release the explosive rope, discharge ballast, and abandon for the present the idea of this experiment, *the balloon exploded*.

"It was a moment of awful suspense. Gas rushed from the rupture in the top of the balloon with a tempestuous noise, and in less than ten seconds not a particle of hydrogen remained in it. The descent at first was rapid, accompanied with a fearful moaning noise caused by the air rushing through the network and the gas escaping above. In another moment I felt a slight shock.

"I looked up; the balloon was canting over, being nicely doubled in, the lower half into the upper. The weight of the car gave it an oscillating motion, which it retained until it reached the earth."

After the lower half of the balloon collapsed into the upper half, the deflated balloon formed a parachute shape. The balloon floated down, oscillating back and forth, until it struck the earth and catapulted Wise out to a safe landing in a clump of bushes.

At very high altitudes without an oxygen supply

Another type of peril survived by a few lucky pioneer balloonists occurred while making flights to very high altitudes, unaware that the lack of oxygen could be fatal. In 1862, two Englishmen, James Glaisher and Henry Coxwell, took a wild balloon ride in an open basket to an altitude which they estimated to be about thirty-seven thousand feet. From what is now known about the effects of high altitude on the human body, it seems impossible that they could have survived at such a great height, but even though their actual maximum altitude was probably lower, the lack of oxygen came extremely close to killing both men. Glaisher noted his sensations as the balloon floated up into very thin air.

"I then looked at the barometer, and found its reading to be nine-and-three-quarters inches, still decreasing fast, implying a height exceeding twenty-nine thousand feet [according to modern tables, nine-and-three-quarters inches of mercury would correspond to 27,800 feet]. Shortly after, I laid my arm upon the table, possessed of its full vigor, but on being desirous of using it, I found it powerless—it must have lost its power momentarily. Trying to move the other arm I found it powerless also. Then I tried to shake myself, and succeeded, but I seemed to have no limbs. In looking at the barometer, my head fell over my left shoulder; I struggled and shook my body again, but could not move my arms. Getting my head upright for an instant only, it fell on my right shoulder. Then I fell backward, my back resting on the side of the car and my head on its edge. In this position my eyes were directed to Mr. Coxwell in the ring. When I shook my body I seemed to have full power over the muscles of the back, and considerably so over those of the neck, but none over either my arms or legs. As in the case of the arms, so all muscular power was lost in an instant from my back and neck. I dimly saw Mr. Coxwell, and endeavored to speak, but could not. In an instant, intense darkness overcame me, so that the optic nerve lost power suddenly, but I was still conscious, with as active a brain as at the present moment of writing this. I thought I had been seized with asphyxia and believed I should experience nothing more, as death would come unless we speedily descended; other thoughts were entering my mind, when I suddenly became unconscious, as on going to sleep."

Coxwell, barely conscious and half-frozen, climbed the balloon's rigging to try to free the valve cord tangled in the shrouds. Because his hands were frost-bitten, Coxwell had to pull the valve line with his teeth, starting the balloon's descent to earth barely in time. Then he collapsed.

The balloon floated down toward earth with its two unconscious passengers. When the two men revived in the lower air, understandably, both had throbbing headaches.

Although unconscious passengers in a balloon can float safely down to earth, an unconscious pilot in a single-seat fighter plane may easily crash before reviving. In 1951 a blacked-out jet pilot was rescued over Korea by two other airplanes using their wings to guide him home.

Capt. John Paladino was flying a single-seat F-84 in formation with two other planes when suddenly his oxygen supply failed and he lost consciousness at thirty-two thousand feet. He later told war correspondents how it felt to black out.

"I was flight leader that day and we were returning from a routine job. There was another flight of F-84s on their way home ahead of us, so I started to lead mine out of the way. You never know when you're not getting enough oxygen; in fact you feel wonderful—sort of rocked, like on vodka. Your coordination and reasoning are off a little, but you feel right up to par. That's how I felt, until it was too late to do anything about it. The first I knew I was in trouble was when I lost my vision and I couldn't see the flight ahead of us. That's all I remember."

When Paladino's oxygen supply first failed he began to fly erratically, diving and then climbing and finally leveling off, a few degrees off course. One of his wing men radioed Paladino to ask if he was allright and Paladino answered, "Yes, I'm okay." Then suddenly the wing man saw Paladino slump forward and he immediately guessed what was wrong.

The two pilots flying in formation with Paladino knew that he was in danger of falling into a spin that might cause him to crash before he could regain consciousness at a lower altitude. They decided that they might be able to keep Paladino's plane level until he could revive if each of them put a wing under one of Paladino's wings. They could do this without actually touching Paladino's wings because the stiff cushions of air flowing over their wingtips did the actual job of supporting his wings.

The two pilots used their planes to guide Paladino's fighter downward toward breathable air. For fifteen minutes they held his plane level, traveling a hundred miles until they had descended to fifteen thousand feet where he was finally able to breathe fairly dense air. Then, at 13,500 feet his eyes opened and he snapped awake. After Paladino landed, his face was deep purple and he had an excruciating headache.

A phenomenal survival of exposure to very thin air and extreme cold at a great altitude was that of a twenty-two-year-old Cuban who escaped from his country and flew to Spain in 1969 as a stowaway in the landing-gear well of a Boeing 707 airliner. Armando Socarras, then twenty-two, dashed out of tall grass beside the runway of Havana's airport and climbed into the right landing gear well of a jetliner readying for takeoff. His friend, sixteen-year-old Jorge Perez, climbed into the left landing gear well.

As the plane lifted into the air, Socarras grabbed some cables and squeezed himself as far up as possible to avoid being crushed by the huge double wheels when they were retracted. Shortly after takeoff the pilot, in response to a light indicating that something was wrong in the wheel well, lowered and retracted the landing gear again. Socarras was able to hang on, but Jorge Perez may have fallen out of the wheel well—he was never seen again. (Perez may have fallen out when the landing gear was lowered for the landing in Madrid.)

Socarras was dressed in a cotton shirt and trousers and he soon began to feel the bite of the cold. "Little by little I felt cold, sleepy, and had great pains in my ears. I must have fallen asleep. I don't know anything more. I know that I woke up once thinking it was terribly cold."

It is no wonder that the lightly clad Socarras felt cold. The nine-hour flight from Havana to Madrid was made at thirty thousand feet where temperatures dropped as low as minus forty degrees Fahrenheit.

When the plane pulled up to a ramp at Madrid's airport, mechanics were startled to see an ice-coated body drop onto the tarmac from the landing gear well. The unconscious Socarras was rushed to a hospital where doctors soaked his arms and legs in warm water to overcome frostbite. Soon he regained consciousness.

How had Socarras survived his ordeal? Climbers have struggled to the top of Mt. Everest, 29,028 above sea level, without breathing oxygen from portable tanks, but their bodies had become adjusted to the thin air over a period of days. For fliers, the U.S. Air Force considers 20,000 to 23,000 feet to be the critical stage where consciousness is lost. During World war II air crewmen in bombers sometimes died when their oxygen supplies failed for less than a half hour at thirty thousand feet, the same altitude at which Socarras survived for nine hours.

The fierce cold may have allowed Socarras to survive in the oxygen-thin air. When his body temperature was lowered—it was ninety-three degrees, or almost six degrees below normal, when he arrived at the hospital—his metabolism slowed down and his brain's need for oxygen was reduced. Also the air pressure inside the wheel housing may have been greater than outside the plane, providing Socarras with enough oxygen to keep him alive. And even though the air temperature was minus forty degrees Fahrenheit outside the plane, Socarras may have been warmed by some of the lingering heat from the wheels and brakes produced by friction during takeoff.

Landing with nobody at the controls

To end our look at harrowing flights that allowed safe landings, let's consider some landings which were made without the pilot at the controls. From time to time pilots of light airplanes lose consciousness and the planes are safely landed, with the help of radioed instructions from a control tower, by nonpilots who are aboard as passengers. Even more amazing, however, are instances where planes have landed themselves safely with no one at the controls.

A U.S. Navy pilot and his passenger became lost in a propeller-driven trainer during a nighttime flight from Norfolk, Virginia, to Washington, D.C. The plane's radio wasn't working, and after a futile search for a place to land, the two men bailed out just as the plane was running out of fuel.

As the pilot drifted down under his chute, the circling pilotless plane kept going around and around him, twice missing him by what seemed like a few feet. The other man's chute brought him down in a big tree and he broke branches all the way to the ground. Both men were unhurt, and so was their airplane. It made a fine landing by itself and was later found undamaged in a field.

An especially unique pilotless landing took place in Egypt during World War II. A B-17 named *Benancye Second* was bringing its American crew back to Cairo after a long mission, when a sudden sandstorm propelled by winds in excess of fifty miles per hour completely blotted out their airfield. The control tower told them to circle overhead while a check was made of other possible landing sites within range of the bomber's dwindling fuel supply. Soon it became clear that all the other available airbases were also unusable because of the same sandstorm.

The plane continued to circle its base in the hope that a momentary lull in the storm might allow a quick landing. However, the impenetrable storm didn't let up and the tower finally ordered the crew to climb to a safe altitude, fly away from Cairo, and then bail out.

When all the fuel gauges showed "empty," the pilot ordered the crew to abandon ship, with each man carrying a knife to cut himself free of his parachute when he hit the ground. Just before the pilot bailed out he set the automatic pilot to carry the plane away from Cairo so it would crash in the open desert. But *Benancye Second* was to come down to a far better fate than most of her crew.

It was very difficult for a pilot to belly land a twenty-ton B-17 even in ideal conditions. But making a landing in a sandstorm with hurricane-force winds, while running out of gas at the exact instant that the throttles had to be cut, and without a pilot at the controls was seemingly impossible. Yet the B-17 did exactly that.

Three days later when the sandstorm had finished, an Egyptian farmer found the plane sitting on his land. *Benancye* had slashed through several acres of cotton and wheat, nimbly threaded her way through a dozen large palms, jumped a ten-foot ditch, and finally stopped in a patch of cotton.

Most B-17s that belly-landed had to be junked and used for spare parts. *Benancye* had made such a perfect landing that except for bent propellers and the sand that was choking her, she was ready to fly again.

The U.S. Army paid the farmer for his crops, and then scraped a runway for the plane across his fields. After mechanics cleaned the sand out of the engine and gave the plane new propellers, it was ready to go. With live pilots at the controls, the plane took off and returned to duty. Her former crew was not so lucky. Most of them had not been able to free themselves from their chutes in time and had been dragged to their deaths across miles of abrasive sand.

CHAPTER 10

Sunk in Subs

During the American Civil War, the Confederacy, plagued by blockading northern ships, decided to build a submarine for underwater attacks on the U.S. Navy gunboats. The submarine was built in Mobile, Alabama, and christened the *H. L. Hunley*, after Horace L. Hunley, a New Orleans cotton merchant who designed the sub and also provided the financial backing to build it. The *Hunley* was basically the metal shell of a cylindrical steel boiler, thirty feet long and enclosed on the ends by a tapered bow and stern. Under ideal conditions the sub could make four knots, powered by its eight crewmen hand-cranking a propeller shaft.

Early in 1863 the *Hunley* began tests in Mobile Bay. During one trial the craft failed to surface. After a frantic search the sub was located and divers and tugs finally brought it to the surface. But it was too late for the eight crewmen—all had suffocated.

Undaunted, the Confederate Navy sent the *Hunley* by rail to Charleston in the summer of 1863 where it was to attack blockading federal warships. On August 29, while cruising on the surface of the Charleston Harbor, the *Hunley* passed too near a paddle steamer. The steamer's wash rolled over the sub's low deck, and before the hatches could be closed, the water poured into the craft and sank it, drowning the entire crew.

The stalwart Confederates persisted and raised the sub again to proceed with their tests. In a short time disaster struck when the sub nosed down into the muddy bottom of the harbor at an angle of forty-five degrees. The sub remained stuck for several days, not having the power to work itself free, and another eight-man crew died.

After the sub was brought to the surface again, it was used in a final training attack on the Confederate ship, *Indian Chief*. The *Hunley* struck the *Indian Chief*'s anchor chain, was thrown out of control, and once again carried the entire crew to their deaths at the bottom of the harbor. This time, Horace L. Hunley himself died in the unreliable submarine.

The *Hunley* was refloated again and finally made ready for action. By now the submarine had become known as "the coffin," and it was very difficult to get a crew of experienced seamen to operate it. The command of the sub was given to a footloose infantry lieutenant, G. E. Dixon. Five soldiers and an officer from the twenty-first South Carolina Infantry were the only volunteers who could be found to serve as crewmen.

The *Hunley* and her insanely brave crew set out on a moonlit night in February 1864 to attack the blockading federal warship *Housatonic*. The crewmen strained at their crankshaft in the shadowy light of swinging oil lamps, propelling the *Hunley* through Charleston harbor with its deck just breaking the surface. As a safety precaution P. G. T. Beauregard, the commanding general at Charleston, had prohibited the *Hunley* from submerging entirely.

The sub had no reliable torpedo to fire at the *Housatonic* but instead had a long wooden spar projecting out from the bow with a mine on the end. As the sub approached the federal gunboat, Lieutenant Dixon ordered the *Hunley*'s lamps extinguished to escape detection. However, a lookout on the federal warship spotted the sub in the moonlight when it was still one hundred yards away. Sailors on the

Housatonic ran to her cannons but they found that the submarine was so close that they couldn't lower the cannons of the federal gunboat far enough to hit the sub.

The *Hunley*'s crew desperately cranked their propeller shaft as the U.S. sailors peppered the sub's deck with musket fire. The sub reached its goal and drove the explosive-tipped spar into the side of the *Housatonic*. The mine exploded, detonating the *Housatonic*'s powder magazine, and the federal ship soon sank to the bottom of the harbor.

The *Housatonic* sank upright and only two officers and three men were lost. The other federal seamen climbed up into the masts, which extended out of the water. The *Hunley* was the first submarine to sink a ship, but the sub's crewmen were not so fortunate as their federal victims. The submarine, carried by the rush of water into the hole blown in the *Housatonic*'s side, was dragged to the bottom with the sinking ship. Once again there were no survivors and the *Hunley* remained on the bottom of the harbor for the rest of the war.

Coping with the perils of primitive submarines

The history of submarines for many decades after the *Hunley* disasters was marked by large numbers of spectacular accidents. These were often caused by various shortcomings in the designs of the early subs.

In the late 1880s Thorsten Nordenfelt, a Swedish arms manufacturer, built a steam-powered submarine which was so unstable that it terrified its own crewmen when demonstrated for prospective buyers in the harbor of Constantinople, Turkey. The following account shows the reason for the crewmen's alarm.

"No sooner did one of the crew take two steps forward in the engine room than down went the bow, whereupon the hot water in the steam boilers and the cold water in the ballast tanks all ran downhill, increasing the slant still further. English engineers, Turkish engineers, monkey wrenches, hot ashes from the boiler fires, Whitehead torpedoes, and other moveables came tumbling after, till the submarine was nearly standing on her head, with everything inside packed into the bow like toys in the toe of a Christmas stocking.

"The crew pulled themselves out of this mess and clawed their way aft, till suddenly up came the bow, down went the stern, and everything went gurgling and clattering to the end.

"The submarine was a perpetual seesaw, and no mortal power could keep her on an even keel. Once they succeeded in steadying her long enough to fire a torpedo. Where it went no man could tell, but the sudden lightening of the bow and the recoil of the discharge made the submarine rear up and sit down so hard that she began to sink stern foremost, whereupon to correct this condition the water was blown out of her ballast tanks by steam pressure, and the main engine started full speed ahead, till she shot up to the surface like a flying fish.

"The Turkish naval authorities, watching the trial from the shores of the Golden Horn, were so impressed by these antics that they bought the boat. But it was impossible to keep a crew on her, for every native engineer or seaman who was sent aboard prudently deserted on the first dark night."

"Swede" Momsen, a very resourceful submarine commander who later won fame by inventing an escape device for trapped submariners called the *Momsen lung*, managed an ingenious escape from the bottom of the Caribbean in 1922 after his out-of-control submarine suddenly plunged to the bottom and stuck fast in the mud. With the bow buried in the mud Momsen ordered the torpedo tubes flooded. This done, Momsen ordered the water blasted out of the tubes with compressed air and the sub was shot free from the muddy bottom.

Another great threat in primitive submarines was the buildup of dangerous gases inside the hull. Submarines trapped on the bottom become filled with high concentrations of carbon dioxide exhaled by the crewmen. When the carbon dioxide reaches seven percent (the normal amount in the atmosphere is only about one-thirtieth of one percent), it is fatal.

Another source of deadly gases in submarines was the battery cells. (Batteries with large storage capacities were needed because most non-nuclear twentieth century subs were powered by electric motors when underwater.) The batteries produced hydrogen gas—tasteless, odorless, and invisible—and when the concentration of this very flammable gas reached four percent it could explode with disastrous consequences for the crew.

Another deadly gas dreaded by the old submariners was chlorine. If sea water leaked into the battery cells, the salt combined with the sulfuric acid in the battery to produce vapors of this yellow-green, suffocating gas. One part of chlorine mixed with 4,999 parts of air was all it took to kill a submarine crewman. Chlorine gas is so deadly that it was the first poison gas used in the gas attacks of World War I.

Some early submarines were driven by gasoline engines (later superceded by oil-burning diesel engines) when cruising on the ocean surface, and escaping gasoline fumes ignited by sparks often exploded and killed crewmen. When the gasoline fumes were inhaled in large quantities, crewmen lost consciousness, but when breathed in lesser amounts the vapors caused a form of intoxication which could have amusing results. Charles Lockwood described the effects of gasoline fumes on a crew under his command in his book, *Hell at 50 Fathoms*. The men were making a submerged run in Manila Bay in 1916 when Commander Lockwood noticed gasoline vapors. They found a leak in a gas line and a puddle on the deck. The crew mopped up the gas with cotton waste, put the waste in a bucket, and covered it with sand, but they were too late—the boat was already filled with fumes.

Rather than surfacing to fill the sub with fresh air, Lockwood stubbornly continued the submerged run. He suddenly lost his view through the periscope as it dipped under the ocean surface. He glanced at the diving rudder man and saw the reason. The diving rudder man was spinning the wheel up and down causing the boat to behave like a "playful porpoise." "Bring her up," Lockwood ordered, "and hold her steady." The diving rudder man turned with a wide grin on his face and replied, "She ain't handlin' right today, Cap'n."

Just then Lockwood heard a snicker behind him, and looking back he saw a sailor at the hand-pump station pumping his arms back and forth as though working the pump—but he was empty-handed.

After ordering the man at the hand pump to stop his foolishness, Lockwood saw his chief's machinist mate coming toward him with a huge smile. "Cap'n," the man said, "that forward main motor bearing is just hotter than hell," and then burst into a laugh. Lockwood rushed to the engine room and witnessed another strange scene when he found "another machinist's mate humming to himself and pouring oil back and forth between two oil cans like an old-fashioned bartender mixing a drink." Lockwood added that, "Even I had to laugh at that scene."

Finally the fumes began to affect Lockwood's brain.

"I told them to give the bearings plenty of oil and hurried back to the periscope. The bay was covered with gentle wavelets. As I looked, the troughs seemed to close over the top, forming tiny balloons that floated off into space, and I seemed to be floating with them. This was too much for me. Groggily, I turned to the electrician at the switchboard and told him not to pull any switch when I ordered surface. I feared a spark might jump from those old-fashioned knife blade switches and blow us all to kingdom come. Then I gave the orders to 'blow the main ballast and bring her up.'"

After the crew reached the surface and fresh air they experienced the fierce headaches that characteristically follow gasoline intoxication.

Another threat in old-fashioned subs was the system of pipes which allowed air to enter a sub when it was on the surface. (Modern nuclear subs can remain submerged indefinitely in contrast to earlier types of subs, because nuclear reactors, unlike diesel or gasoline engines, do not need oxygen, so oxygen can be stored and purified for the crew.) If a valve on an air intake was inadvertently left open or stuck open when a sub dived, water could pour in and sink the craft.

Clever thinking in sunken submarines

In 1920, an open valve allowed the sea to rush into the U.S. submarine *S-5*, sinking the boat fifty miles off the Delaware coast in 183 feet of water. Though the flow was stopped short of completely filling the sub there was a long, desperate struggle by the thirty-seven submariners aboard to save themselves. The sub's skipper, Lt. Comdr. Charles M. Cooke, Jr., knew that there was no way to communicate with the surface. They couldn't expect anyone to begin searching for them for two days, and even after a search began it would be virtually impossible to find the submarine. They would die by asphyxiation in approximately two days unless they could reach fresh air. Cooke, nicknamed "Savvy" by his 1910 Annapolis classmates, would need every bit of his ingenuity to get out of this fix.

The crew would have to save themselves, and Cooke could think of only one way to do that. The sub, resting in 183 feet of water, was 231 feet long, and although the bow was too flooded to budge off the bottom, Cooke figured that by blowing the water out of the sub's after main ballast tank, the stern should rise almost vertically and stick out of the water. Then the crew might be able to drill a hole through the stern to reach fresh air.

To get the stern up out of the water the crew would have to lighten the boat by getting all the weight out that could be ejected. Then they would have to try to break the suction that held the boat's hull fast to the mud. They ejected fuel oil, used compressed air to blow water out of the ballast tanks, and reversed the one remaining good motor to break the suction. The stern came free from the mud and began to rise, but it stopped, still hanging in the water. Cooke ordered the doors to the rear compartments opened, allowing water which had accumulated in these areas to flood down through the boat to the bow. The stern moved up more, and when the motor was started again the stern finally shot up out of the water. Tools, equipment, and men all came crashing down toward the bow of the submarine. One man nearly drowned before he could be pulled out of the flooded forward part of the boat.

Now a new deadly peril threatened the men—chlorine gas. After the sub sank, the battery room in the forward part of the boat contained a large amount of water, but the seawater had not yet entered the battery tanks to form the lethal gas. However, when the sub tilted up near the vertical, the downrushing water hit the batteries and they began to spew out chlorine gas.

The men hurried out of the battery room and closed its door, but debris had collected in the door fittings and poison gas continued to seep out of the compartment. To escape, the men had to grasp anything that would hold them and pull themselves up into the compartments near the stern of the sub; the boat was sticking up at an angle of seventy-five degrees. Shutting compartment doors between themselves and the battery room, they managed to escape from the gas.

The men were now faced with the problem of drilling a hole through the three-quarter inch tempered steel that made up the sub's hull. Cooke climbed up into the very tail of the boat—the eighteen-foot-long tiller room—and by tapping he estimated that about seventeen feet of the sub stuck above water. The crew located an electric drill to make a hole for fresh air, but they soon discovered that they had no power supply. Someone would have to go down into the poisonous battery room to get a battery to run the drill.

An officer volunteered to go for a battery, made himself a makeshift gas mask, and succeeded in returning with a battery—only to find that he had brought back a dead battery. A seaman volunteered to go for another battery, brought back a live one, and the drilling began.

The crewmen, working in soaking wet clothes with the

poorly grounded drill, suffered excruciating shocks as a large part of the current passed through the body of whoever was operating the drill. They took turns, working in total darkness, as all the other men sat still and silent to preserve oxygen. The ship had sunk at 2 P.M. on September 1; by dawn of the next day the men had drilled a triangular hole about three or four inches wide. Cooke saw a ship through the tiny hole, but it passed by without giving any sign that it had seen the sub's exposed stern.

The men enlarged the hole very slowly with the drill until their power plant failed. Then they used hacksaw blades and chisels—working in one or two minute shifts because the air was steadily worsening in the sub despite the tiny hole—to increase the size to about five by six inches by noon. The crewmen were so exhausted from their desperate work in the foul air that it seemed impossible for them to make the hole any larger.

Suddenly the man working at the hole saw a ship about two miles away. Cooke called for a piece of pipe and some oily rags to wrap around its end. He planned to set fire to the rags and attract the ship by signaling it with the smoke. No one could find a dry match and as Cooke waved the pipe and unlit rags the ship sailed away.

Finally at 2 P.M. a young seaman working at the hole shouted, "Hold your hats! Steamboat coming round the bend!" The same ship they had seen at noon—a dilapidated freighter—had come back thinking that the submarine's stern was a buoy. The freighter's captain figured that he was off course and came back to try to identify the buoy.

The freighter stopped near the upended sub, a boat was lowered, and the freighter's captain was rowed to the strange-looking object sticking out of the sea. "Capt. Edward Johnson of the steamer *Alanthus*," he identified himself and then asked, "What ship is this?" "The submarine *S-5*, U.S. Navy," answered Cooke. "What is your destination?" questioned the captain, sticking to the language of formal protocol. Seeing the humor in the situation, Cooke answered, "Hell, by compass!" and broke into a laugh.

Johnson expressed his regrets over the submarine's predicament and set out to save the lives of the submariners. The air in the sub was dangerously foul, the temperature had risen to 120 degrees, and the supplies of drinking water had long since been exhausted. The freighter's radioman had missed the boat in the last port and no one else knew how to run the radio so they could not call for help. Also, the freighter lacked any but the most rudimentary cutting tools. However, the freighter could supply drinking water and fresh air. Water was brought in buckets from the ship and poured through the hole with the help of a funnel and a hose. It was caught by the men in the sub and passed around. The freighter then crept up close to the sub and secured its upright position by fastening cables to the upraised stern and drawing them tight. A washdeck hose was attached to one of the freighter's deck pumps, passed through the hole, and lowered down into the sub. The sailors on the freighter then pumped fresh air down into the sub, quickly reviving the submarine crewmen.

The freighter crewmen then furiously attacked the hole with bits, drills, and chisels until they had it large enough for a man to pass through by 1 A.M. on September 3. By 3:34 A.M., Cooke, the last man to leave the sub, was hoisted aboard the freighter.

Earlier the freighter had sent signals of distress, which were seen by a passing ocean liner and radioed to the U.S. Navy. A battleship arrived to try to tow the partly flooded sub into port, but high seas and bad weather caused the sub to slip away from the battleship before reaching the Delaware coast. The Navy spent months trying to raise the *S-5*, but unlike her crew, the sub never reached port again.

In December 1921 the U.S. submarine *S-48*, with forty-one men aboard, found itself in a similar predicament to that of the *S-5*, except that the *S-48* was held down after sinking by a flooded stern rather than a flooded bow. A careless workman had not fastened down a cover in the newly built submarine, and this allowed water to rush directly from a main ballast tank into the engine room.

The captain, Joseph Austin, remembering how Cooke had saved the crew of the *S-5* the previous year, realized that in this case he would have to raise the sub's bow above water while the stern rested on the bottom. No one had seen the sub sink and rescuers wouldn't be able to find her unless at least a part of the sub reappeared above the sea. Because the submarine was 240 feet long and had sunk in seventy-five feet of water this would seem easy, but unfortunately the *S-48* contained a greater tonnage of water than the *S-5*. The crew moved all portable equipment aft and blew the forward ballast tanks, but although the bow came up it didn't raise above the ocean's surface.

At this time chlorine gas began to waft through the boat from the sulfuric acid that had slopped over from the battery cells and mixed with sea water. Chief Electricians Mate Mike Fritz found a small rubber hose, cut it into six pieces, kept one piece, and passed out the other five pieces to shipmates. Then the men got down on their knees, pushed the ends of their tubes into the pools of sea water and sulfuric acid under the batteries, put the other ends of the tubes into their mouths, and sucked until the water ran through the tubes. Having established suction, they siphoned the water into coffee mugs and stopped the formation of chlorine gas. The six self-sacrificing men, all working in the dark with only an occasional check-beam from a pocket flashlight, suffered lip and mouth burns from the sulfuric acid.

Now the crew turned their attention back to raising the bow. First they shot two dummy torpedoes to the surface with messages attached to them that read, "Bring help. *S-48* sunk in sixty feet off Penfield Reef." (Although the sub had sunk in water seventy-five feet deep, there were only sixty feet between the top of the sub and the ocean surface.) However, no one ever spotted the torpedoes.

Finally the crew figured out how to raise the bow. The sub had a sounding device to determine the distance to the ocean bottom. This consisted of a double-ended valve, six inches in diameter. The upper end was opened and the bottom one was closed and a lead was dropped into the pipe. Then the upper valve was closed, leaving passage only for the lead line, and the lower valve opened, allowing the lead and its attached line to drop to the ocean bottom to make the sounding. The newly-built submarine—which was undergoing sea trials before being turned over to the Navy—was carrying five tons of pig-iron bars so that it would simulate the weight of a sub prepared for duty. The crew began to drop the pig iron bars through the sounding valve system and this in combination with blowing the after main ballast finally brought the bow above water.

The captain then asked the crew to sit silently and conserve air until a passing ship saw the exposed bow. There would be no attempt to cut a hole through the hull as was done in the S-5. However, Peter J. Dunne, a nineteen-year-old apprentice mechanic who was one of the civilian crewmen supplied by the sub's builder, suddenly had a bright idea. He would climb up a torpedo tube onto the bow.

After receiving the captain's permission, Dunne started up the twenty-three-foot long, twenty-one-inch diameter tube. The tube was larded with heavy grease to ease the loading of torpedoes, and Dunne slipped back many times before reaching the muzzle of the tube. As Dunne climbed up on top of the sub he found himself in a bitter cold night with gale-force winds whipping up the sea fifteen feet below him. He attached the end of the cable he had carried up the tube to a cleat on the outside of the sub, and other men began to use the cable to pull themselves up the tube. After five men were perched on the bow—the captain didn't want too many men on the bow for fear that the bow would submerge like a New England ducking stool—they began to signal frantically for help. First they used a blinker light and then they began to burn anything they could find in a wire wastebasket: books, papers, charts, kapok mattresses from the crew's bunks, etc.

The crew of a passing tugboat, which was pulling a huge barge, spotted the distress signals and directed their searchlight on the object. They were amazed to see a dark object sticking up out of the ocean with a group of men huddling on top. The tug's captain exclaimed, "I'll be damned if I know what it is, who they are, or how they got

there, but I do know that we've got to get them off and
damn pronto. In this wind and sea, they could be swept
away at any moment."

In a great display of seamanship the tug's captain
stopped his barge against the side of the ship's bow. The
five submariners jumped onto the barge, the last one sending a signal down to the crewmen still in the sub that rescue had come. The tug's crew then saved all the remaining
submariners by making repeated trips to the sub with their
rowboat. A few weeks later the *S-48* was salvaged and
towed back to port.

CHAPTER 11

Deliverance from the Depths

Now that we've reviewed various causes of submarine accidents in "the good old days," let's talk about the type of accident that has taken the greatest number of submariner's lives—collisions with other subs or surface ships. If a surface ship is involved in a collision, no matter how serious, it probably won't sink for minutes, or even hours, and those on board can generally escape in lifeboats. A submarine, in contrast, has most of its hull beneath the water and little reserve buoyancy. Even a small rupture of its hull can cause uncontrollable flooding and a sudden plunge to the ocean bottom.

Some subs have escaped collisions by very narrow margins. For example, in 1911 the United States Submarine *Salmon* was making a training dive in Long Island Sound off New London, Connecticut. As the sub was moving along its assigned course underwater it was suddenly shaken violently as if it had struck something. When the *Salmon* surfaced, the skipper saw that a big bell and its supports, which had been located on the bow, were missing. The mystery was solved when someone at submarine headquarters compared the track charts for various submarines that day and learned that another sub had strayed from its assigned course and crossed the path of the *Salmon*, neatly carrying away its deck bell while skimming just above the hull.

During the overcast, moonless night of February 1, 1918, collisions damaged three British submarines and sank two others off the coast of Scotland. These five submarines had been among a group of eight subs that was on its way, along with a large number of British surface ships, to conduct fleet excercises. To avoid detection by German submarines, the British ships were keeping absolute radio silence and were blacked out except for dim white lights at their sterns. Suddenly two small British patrol boats, obviously unaware of the procession of warships, appeared out of the dark causing several submarines to take evasive action. The darkened subs and surface ships veered around blindly, resulting in a series of collisions and near collisions with submarines. One of the British submarines, the *K-12*, headed directly at a British battle cruiser. The thirty-thousand ton battle cruiser and the two-thousand ton submarine, moving toward each other at a relative speed of forty-five miles per hour, swooshed past each other on opposite courses with one yard of open water between. The *K-12* was one of the three submarines to escape a collision during that calamitous, black night.

A very unusual collision nearly sank a sub commanded by Lothar von Arnauld de la Periere who, despite his French surname, was the top scoring German submarine commander, in sinking ships, of World War I. Von Arnauld torpedoed a ship at close range and its momentum carried it over his submarine. The torpedoed ship then sank on top of the sub before von Arnauld could steer clear. The sinking ship tore away the sub's periscope, blinding it, but the submarine managed to work itself free before the sinking hulk carried the sub down and pinned it to the bottom.

Terrifying escapes from sunken subs

British petty officer, William Brown, needed all of his ingenuity and persistence to escape from a sunken sub after a collision sent it to the ocean bottom in August 1916, off the port of Harwich. Brown, who sealed himself in the engine room, was the only crewman in the sub still alive. Water was filling the compartments on both sides of him and he realized that the relatively thin metal bulkheads would probably soon cave in and drown him in a flood of sea water.

To counteract the dangerous pressure differences between the adjacent compartments and his own, Brown opened the engine room speaking tubes to admit water slowly to the engine room. The buildup of water in the engine room reduced the pressure imbalances between the adjacent compartments and took away the threat to the bulkheads, but the rising water level soon reached Brown's knees and then his waist.

Brown began to look for a way out of the sub, but this was not easy because the lights had shorted out except for occasional flickers. He tried every exit, but none would open. As he felt around for an escape route he was repeatedly jolted by shocks coming from the shorted out electric control panel. To add to the horror he began to smell choking fumes of chlorine gas from the flooded propulsion batteries.

Brown quickly thought of a method of escape that was just the opposite of his natural inclination to hold off the sea water that was threatening to drown him. Overhead was a hatch, used to bring torpedoes into the boat, which opened up out of the sub. Brown had tried to lift it, but the enormous pressure of sea water outside the submarine held it tightly shut. Brown reasoned that if he let enough water into the engine compartment, the air pressure inside would increase until it was nearly equal to the pressure of the sea water outside and he could lift the hatch.

Brown opened the valves to increase the flow of sea water into the compartment and the pressure of the air in the engine room increased as the water level rose. Suddenly, before Brown was ready to escape, the increased air pressure pushed the hatch open slightly and a large bubble of air escaped up into the sea. This reduced the air pressure in the compartment and the hatch clanged shut tightly once again.

Brown studied the hatch with his fingertips and found that there was a retaining pin in place that would allow it to rise only a few inches—enough to allow air to escape, but not enough to let him escape even after pressure built up again in the engine room. The only way to release the pin was to turn a gear on the deck near his feet which controlled it. He dove underwater and moved the gear, releasing the pin.

As water continued to pour into the compartment, air pressure built up once again and Brown looked forward to what he thought would be his imminent escape. However each time the pressure built up the air would escape in a quick spurt and the hatch would fall shut again.

Brown decided that he needed to keep the hatch fastened until pressure built up to a great amount, and then suddenly release the hatch so he could be blown out of the sub by the pressure. He found two clip bolts, fastened them to the hatch to hold it in place, and let the pressure increase. Then he knocked the bolts away. The pressure was still not great enough to blow the hatch clear open, however, and the hatch slammed back down, smashing onto one of Brown's hands.

The persistent Brown then tried to escape once more, removing some heavy plates that had closed off openings in the sub's hull to allow even more water into the compartment. The water rose until only Brown's face, turned up almost against the hatch, was out of water. This certainly would be his last possible chance to escape. Brown knocked the clip bolts loose with his uninjured hand and a great rush of pressure blew the hatch clear open. Brown floated to the surface where a British destroyer fished him out of the water. He had worked for nearly two hours—including six futile attempts to open the hatch—before he finally escaped.

Brown was not the first submariner to figure out that he would have to flood his compartment and increase air pressure in order to open a hatch and escape from a sunken submarine. In 1851 Wilhelm Bauer, a German artilleryman, was demonstrating a primitive submarine powered by two hand-operated tread wheels in the hope that the German states would buy it. However, the demonstration was a disaster, and Bauer and his two crewmen sank to the bottom of Kiel harbor, coming to rest fifty-two feet underwater. Bauer explained to the two men that they needed to let more water into the sub so that they could open the hatch and escape. The two crewmen, standing in frigid water up to their chests, weren't convinced. They began to work their hand pumps furiously to force the water out. Bauer, afraid that the two men would be too exhausted to swim when the time came for escape, opened the cocks wide and water began to flood the boat. The two crewmen begged Bauer not to drown them and then one of the men, crazed by fear, rushed at Bauer with a knife. Bauer stopped the panic-stricken sailor by drawing his revolver, even though the weapon was too wet to fire.

After the pressure had built up in the sub, one of the crewmen started to raise the hatch, but terrified by the onrush of water, he let it slam shut. Bauer ordered the understandably reluctant man to raise the hatch clear up and the surge of escaping air propelled all three men toward the surface. Bauer and the two others bobbed up right in the middle of the funeral service being held for them. At first the mourners were speechless, and then they began to shout joyously.

Floating up to the surface from sunken submarines involves considerable risk, especially if the sub is in fairly deep water. The air must be exhaled slowly at first and then in steadily increasing volumes as the escaper ascends. Otherwise, pressure that can tear lung tissue will be built up in the lungs. This pressure can cause hemorrhaging in the lungs or force air into the blood stream, producing air bubbles and an air embolism. These results can be fatal. There have been cases of air embolism with ascents from depths as shallow as ten feet. During an ascent to the water surface, one should exhale enough so that there is never any feeling of distention in the chest.

When submariners have been breathing air under high pressure before making an ascent—as is necessary when increasing pressure in order to open a hatch—dangerous amounts of nitrogen, the most abundant element in air, may be forced into blood and tissue. If the escaper ascends too rapidly from a depth of greater than one hundred feet, the nitrogen can form bubbles in the tissues. In severe cases this causes terrible pain in the limbs and abdomen, and the victim may double up ("the bends"). Other symptoms are "staggers" (vertigo), "chokes" (asphyxia), and even unconsciousness. A human suffering from the horrors of the bends could well envy the ability of seals to avoid these effects. Seals can dive as far as fifteen hundred feet below the surface and bob back up painlessly and they do this up to twenty times each day. They avoid high levels of nitrogen gas in their lungs by exhaling before they plunge, completely collapsing their lungs in mid-dive and dispersing any residual nitrogen throughout their muscles and thick blubber layer. Blubber can dissolve more than four times the nitrogen that blood can.

Deepest unaided escape

The record for the greatest depth of an unaided, emergency escape from a submarine is held by Dr. Richard A. Slater, who ascended from an estimated 225 feet in 1970. Slater and another man were in a two-man submarine helping to raise a sunken speed boat near Catalina Island off the coast of California. They used the sub's mechanical arm to tie lines to the sunken boat, and as the speed boat was being lifted by a large ship on the surface, the sub began its ascent. However, the speed boat slipped off its lines, dropped back down through the sea, and landed on the sub. The falling speed boat cracked the Plexiglas porthole beside Slater's face and the sea smashed through the weakened viewport, shooting Plexiglas fragments into the right side of Slater's face.

Slater was knocked unconscious by the blow on the side of his head, but soon he was revived by the cold water pouring in on him. The rush of water into the sub soon caused the inside pressure to equalize the outside pressure and Slater knew that he would have to get out immediately.

"It was all very dreamy, but I remember taking a last breath of air before the sub filled with water, and then I remember opening the hatch. The sub had landed at a forty-five-degree angle, so we had to crawl out sideways. As I got ready to leave, the rear pocket of my jeans caught on the rudder control knob. I remember thinking that I had a long way to go and that I was stuck.

"Then I pushed off. The pocket of my jeans was found later in the sub; I had ripped the rivets right out of my pants.

"I don't remember much about coming up.

"There was never any panic. Both of us were very experienced divers so we knew what to do by instinct.

"I remember thinking, 'It's a long way up, it's a long way to go.'"

Slater blew out air as he floated up. The air he had inhaled in the submarine would expand about eight times by the time he reached the surface. It had taken him somewhere between three and five minutes to reach the surface. Slater was unconscious when he bobbed up about twenty feet from two men in a dinghy. These two men had become bored, left the main ship in its row boat, and rowed over to a kelp bed to do some fishing. The large ship was about one hundred yards away from where Slater had surfaced. If the two men had not been close by in the rowboat, no one would have ever seen him and he would gradually have gone back down.

After they lifted the unconscious Slater into their boat, they saw blood coming from his mouth and assumed that his lungs had burst. The blood was actually coming from the cuts in his cheek, a couple of which extended clear into his mouth. He was not breathing.

The apparently dead Slater was moved from the dinghy to a water-ski boat for a fast trip to the water-accident oriented hospital at Avalon on Catalina Island. One man in the water-ski boat wanted to give Slater mouth-to-mouth resuscitation, but he couldn't find Slater's mouth—there was too much gore. It was a choppy day and the ski boat bounced violently. Slater, lying on the bottom of the boat, suddenly vomited and began to breathe. He figured that the bouncing must have had the effect of artificial respiration.

Slater regained consciousness several hours later in the hospital. His eardrums had been blown out and he couldn't hear. However, his eardrums gradually grew back and his hearing returned to normal. He later became a professor of geology at the University of Northern Colorado. The other sub crewman was not so lucky—he never made it to the surface alive.

Some submariners—unlike those in our examples—have escaped from sunken subs while wearing specially developed types of portable breathing apparatuses. Also, escape locks, consisting of chambers with watertight doors, were built into subs to serve as escape exits for trapped crewmen.

Escapes in rescue chambers

Rescues of sub crewmen from extreme depths can be made with a special rescue chamber, ten feet high, eight feet in diameter, and weighing ten tons, which is lowered from a ship to the deck of a sunken sub. Rescuers in the chamber then link a gasketed skirt at the bottom of the chamber to the submarine's escape hatch and trapped submariners climb up into the rescue vessel. If the sea surface is relatively calm and if the sub is oriented so that the chamber can land on its escape hatch, rescues can be made from depths as great as 800 to 850 feet.

In 1939 the United States submarine *Squalus* sank in 240 feet of water. Thiry-three seamen were alive but trapped in the forward torpedo room, and twenty-nine other men were trapped and drowned in compartments nearer the stern. An early version of the rescue chamber made four trips down to the rescue hatch of the sub and saved all of the surviving crewmen.

Trapped in sunken ships

Crewmen have been rescued, not only from sunken submarines, but sometimes from inside ships after they have sunk. Sunken ships often contain small, isolated pockets of air and some extremely lucky sinking victims have managed to reach a lifesaving bubble of air and survive until freed by divers.

At 3:46 A.M. on a November morning in 1980, a 465-foot tanker crashed into the side of a 120-foot oil field workboat on the Mississippi River. The workboat rolled on its side with its keel broken by the impact and soon sank below the river's surface. Wrapped around the tanker's bow, it was pushed ahead of the large ship underwater at nearly seventeen miles per hour. The tanker's captain wanted to lower his anchors and stop, but the position of the wrecked workboat on his bow made it impossible for the anchors to enter the water. He therefore decided to head for shallow water on the river's west bank where he could ground his ship. At 5:40 A.M., two hours after the collision, the tanker, with the workboat still attached to its bow, eased aground in soft mud about a half mile from shore.

It seemed impossible that any one of its four crewmen could be alive in the flooded hull of the wrecked workboat. One crewman had been drowned immediately in the boat and two others had been swept downriver to their deaths. But Anthony Perret, a nineteen-year-old deck hand, was still alive in the hull. Trapped in his cabin, Perret had suddenly found himself swimming in pitch darkness after the water rushed into the stricken boat. He grabbed onto an overturned steel locker underwater and groped along it until he broke into an air pocket. Feeling his way around the darkness he discovered that the air pocket was only about two feet high and four feet square. He forced himself up into the steel locker and curled into a tight ball to fit. It all seemed very unreal. He wondered if he had died and this was some strange form of life after death.

Perret was terrified by the sounds of the tanker's engines racing, stopping, and then racing again as the captain grounded the ship. Perret imagined that he saw a mangled body floating toward him, but he realized that his mind was playing tricks on him. He remembered the butane lighter in his pocket, pulled it out, and flicked its wheel until it caught. He saw above him what had been the left side of the bow, and he was glad to see no evidence that the water level was rising. He extinguished the lighter to save fuel.

Feelings of terror alternated with feelings of hope as Perret tried to understand his situation. He would have given anything to know where he was and what was happening, but his confusion was only increased by what he heard and felt. The metal groaned and vibrated around him and he heard the rushing sound of turbulent water.

At 7 A.M., over three hours after the accident, a Coast Guard crewman in a small boat, looking for bodies, banged his oar on the hull and thought he heard an answering tap. He banged the oar again and heard a series of short taps in reply. Soon a call went out for divers.

The divers struggled through the wreck to Perret (it was like going through a "big, dark junkyard with the Mississippi River flowing through it"), provided him with scuba gear which he would be using for the first time, and brought him to safety at 11:20 A.M., seven hours and thirty-four minutes after he had first crawled into his tiny air pocket.

Trapped in all sorts of sunken things

Air pockets have saved potential drowning victims not only in sunken ships but also in a variety of other types of sunken objects, such as offshore oil rigs, aircraft, and automobiles. For example, an oil rig being towed to a new worksite sank in 1975, trapping five men below water in the Gulf of Mexico. One man, perched on a large pipe with his head in an eighteen-inch air space, was rescued by divers after spending twenty-two hours in his pitch-black prison. Four other men were saved after spending twenty-six hours clinging to pipes and valves to keep their heads in a foul pocket of air filled with nauseating diesel fumes. Just before they were located by divers, the men were talking about their families, about dying, and where they would be buried. Their only light was a glimmer from a luminous dial on a wristwatch. One of the trapped men later recalled their rescue:

"It was miserable. I had to keep moving and the diesel fumes were almost putting me under. I had just about given up hope. I was drowsy and I propped my head up when all of a sudden there was a light and this diver came out of the water. You never heard such hollering and screaming."

A bubble of air was a lifesaver when Chuck Yeager and his commander, Gen. Irving "Twig" Branch, were picked up by a U.S. Army helicopter after fishing in California's Sierra Nevada Mountains. As their overloaded aircraft took off at about eleven thousand feet, it suddenly flipped over and crashed upside down in the middle of an icy lake. Yeager escaped and began swimming toward the shore. He saw their ice chest pop up to the surface followed by the helicopter's crew chief, then the copilot, and next the pilot. Yeager estimated that three or four minutes passed before General Branch

bobbed up to the surface, gasping for air with his eyes
bulging. Branch had been trapped in the cockpit and he
had to break the Plexiglas and escape from underneath
the helicopter. If it had not been for an air pocket in the
cockpit, Branch would have drowned. Unfortunately, the
next year Branch was killed in an air crash.

Air pockets can also save lives after automobiles sink
underwater. In Florida, a pretty, blonde, seventeen-year-
old girl, seated in a parked car with the windows rolled up,
suddenly found herself fifteen feet underwater after the car
started forward and slipped over a bank into a river. Despite repeated dives by rescuers she remained in the car for
almost fifteen minutes. The door next to her was jammed
shut so she could not escape. She had learned in a lifesaving course that a bubble of air sometimes remains in submerged cars, but after the water level kept rising until it
was over her head she thought that she was going to
drown.

She was able to squeeze from the front seat, past the
head rests, into the back seat, and then she found the bubble of air. By feel she estimated that the air pocket was
about six feet long, two feet wide, and eighteen inches
deep. But water was coming in fast and soon she was huddled back under the rear window with her head tilted up to
raise her nose and mouth into the rapidly disappearing air
bubble. The water was up to her chin. The small remaining
amount of air was slowly turning into suffocating carbon
dioxide, and the girl slapped her own face to stay awake.
However, about ten minutes after the car had gone underwater she blacked out. When a fireman finally pulled her to
the surface about fifteen minutes after the car had submerged, her face was gray and her eyes were closed. He
feared the worst, but at that moment she gasped for air and
shouted "Help me!"

One of the smallest bubbles to sustain life underwater
for an extended period of time was in a water conduit in
Melbourne, Australia. A twelve-year-old boy playing in a
fountain fell down a twelve-foot vertical water-filled shaft
and then was washed along a horizontal tunnel, thrashing

about wildly with his lungs bursting. He bumped into a vertical pipe, held on, and then tried to haul himself up it to fresh air. But his head struck the ceiling and he realized that he was trapped.

He could not hold his breath any longer, but when he inhaled he found that he breathed air rather than water. When he lowered his face he immediately touched water, and moving around the pipe he found that the air pocket surrounded the very top of the pipe, extending out about a foot.

The boy felt the water suddenly become calm around him—rescuers above had stopped the flow of water through the tunnel. Although he didn't realize it, the circulating water had brought the air bubbles that kept him alive and now as he breathed he was rapidly using up his supply of air.

Although it seemed impossible that the boy could still be alive, the rescue team planned to pump out water until there was an inch or two of air space along the ceiling of the horizontal tunnel. Then a man would swim in on his back to the youngster. As the tiny air space appeared the man heard a cry for help. The boy had survived for over an hour and a half in his tiny air bubble. He was rushed to a medical center. He was in good shape except for some abrasions on his hands and legs where the current had brushed him against the tunnel wall.

Narrow escapes of subs in combat

Now, let's go back to submarines and talk about some subs' brushes with disaster in combat. There are innumerable stories about depth charges exploding so close to submarines that hulls began to leak, paint flakes rained down off ceilings, light bulbs and glass covers on dials shattered, and equipment and crewmen were thrown around inside subs. Explosions of depth charges at close range occasionally also imperiled subs by throwing them off course.

Ben Bryant, who survived more patrols than any other World War II British submarine commander, once had his sub hurled toward the surface by depth charges that exploded underneath the boat. The crew desperately flooded ballast tanks to stop the ascent, but the sub still rocketed upward out of control. If they broke surface, the German antisubmarine boats would spot the sub and sink it.

At first it seemed as though nothing could stop the sub from surfacing, but the crew finally stopped the ascent about five feet from the surface. Then the sub, its ballast tanks terribly heavy with water, began to plunge down out of control. If it went too deep the hull would be crushed by the excessive pressure.

The submarine hurtled down past the depth it was designed to withstand with the crew furiously blowing water out of the main ballast tanks. They finally stopped the descent just short of where the hull would have collapsed. Bryant recalled seeing a British submarine that had come even closer to being crushed by sea pressure.

"I saw an S boat (a class of British submarines), *Stubborn*, which had lost control in action and been down to over five hundred feet. Her plating had started to cave in and, though she lived to tell the tale, her ribs were sticking out like a starving race horse. She required extensive rebuilding."

Some submarines also had narrow escapes from underwater mines. Wolfgang Luth, one of the most successful World War II German U-boat commanders, recalled one such reprieve:

"I had, on one patrol, a coxswain who was a nice enough fellow, but had an unfortunate tendency to get rattled. We were making our way through one of our own minefields and I told him, 'Tomorow morning, at 0300, you must begin to zigzag, because it will be starting to get light then and we may encounter enemy submarines. Tomorrow morning at 0500, we will alter course from 300 degrees to 270 degrees.'

"When I got to the bridge at five next morning, I found that he had already altered course without me—two hours before, at the same time he had started to zigzag! After steering for a while on 270, he had then confused port with starboard and gone to 240 for his next leg, instead of to 300. So for two full hours, we had been snaking our way through the middle of a minefield.

"It was a horrible sensation and infuriating to think we might have gone sky-high through a shambles like that. I couldn't refrain from telling him that if we struck a mine, I'd have it in for him in heaven! We turned immediately and made our way back carefully, following the same route."

Many submarines have been sunk by torpedoes fired by enemy submarines. A German submarine had a very improbable escape from a torpedo during World War I. Lt. A. C. Bennett, the commander of the U.S. submarine *L-11*, spotted a German sub on the surface about nine hundred yards away and prepared to attack. Bennett fired two torpedoes at the sub, one right after the other. The two torpedoes seemed to be running fine, but when they were still about two hundred yards from the German sub there was a tremendous explosion. Apparently the second torpedo was running slightly faster than the first and caught up and ran into it, exploding both. The German sub quickly submerged, unharmed.

The German sub U-35 also had an incredibly lucky day during World War I. Prince Sigismund, a nephew of the Kaiser and another officer were standing watch on the conning tower of the surfaced submarine when they saw a periscope nearby. Before they had time to shout a warning, they saw a torpedo headed straight for them—too close to take any action except to watch in horror as their lives came to an end.

The attacking allied sub had apparently set its torpedo to run at a very shallow depth, and this probably explains what happened next. Just before it reached the

U-35, the torpedo porpoised out of the water, passed through the air in the narrow space between the U-boat's conning tower and its deck gun, and then clattered down onto the deck and bounced into the water on the other side. The captain of the sub, Lothar von Arnauld de la Periere, who had a narrow escape earlier in this chapter when a torpedoed ship sank onto his sub, came running up the ladder of the conning tower when he heard the clatter. Seeing the enemy sub's periscope, he gave the order to turn away so that the U-35 would offer only its narrow stern for a target. Almost immediately a second torpedo passed within a few feet of the hull, and before the U-35 could submerge two more enemy torpedoes sped harmlessly by.

CHAPTER 12

Overboard!

*O*ne *of* the most terrifying things associated with sinking ships is the suction which can pull its helpless victims down with the vessel. The fierce currents created when water floods into the remaining air spaces in a foundering ship cause a deadly undertow, but as water fills the ship, the air must escape and some apparently doomed victims have been shot up to safety by a burst of escaping air.

The Reverend H. L. Gwyer and his bride Margaret, a young couple from Edmonton, Canada, were on the *Lusitania* when it was torpedoed off the coast of Ireland by a German submarine on a beautiful spring day in 1915. There were 1,959 passengers and crew members on board, and 1,198 died.

Margaret Gwyer had started to swim as soon as the boat deck sank beneath the ocean, but within a short time she was drawn headfirst by the inrush of water into the mouth of one of the huge funnels. Survivors in a nearby lifeboat, who had been appalled to see Margaret swallowed by the submerged funnel, were then amazed to see her shot out again, like a circus performer hurled out of a cannon. Blackened with soot, she flew through the air and splashed down into the ocean.

Detective Inspector William Pierpoint, the ship's detective, was also swallowed up by a funnel and then spewed out by a mixture of escaping air and black water. The *Lusitania*'s captain observed that Pierpoint, after being shot out of the funnel to safety, was "swimming like ten men, he was so scared."

Margaret Gwyer and William Pierpoint were both rescued and Margaret, still black with soot, recognized her husband in a crowd on the ship that picked her up. At first her husband did not know her as she rushed toward him, but soon they were hugging one another and laughing unbelievingly about their salvation.

Charles H. Lightoller, a short, stocky, efficient officer on the *Titanic*, was nearly drowned by suction before escaping from the sinking liner. After loading women and children aboard lifeboats, Lightoller could see that the *Titanic* was about to start its dive to the ocean bottom and he jumped into the sea.

"Striking the water was like a thousand knives being driven into one's body, and, for a few moments, I completely lost grip of myself—and no wonder, for I was perspiring freely, whilst the temperature of the water was twenty-eight degrees [Fahrenheit], or four degrees below freezing.

"On the boat deck, above our quarters, on the fore part of the forward funnel, was a huge rectangular air shaft and ventilator, with an opening about twenty by fifteen feet. On this opening was a light wire grating to prevent rubbish being drawn down or anything else thrown down. This shaft led direct to No. 3 stokehold, and was therefore a sheer drop of close on one hundred feet, right to the bottom of the ship.

"I suddenly found myself drawn, by the sudden rush of the surface water pouring down this shaft, and held flat and firmly up against this wire netting with the additional full and clear knowledge of what would happen if this light wire carried away. The pressure of the water just glued me there whilst the ship sank slowly below the surface.

"Although I struggled and kicked for all I was worth, it

was impossible to get away, for as fast as I pushed myself off I was irresistibly dragged back, every instant expecting the wire to go and to find myself shot down into the bowels of the ship.

"Apart from that, I was drowning, and a matter of another couple of minutes would have seen me through. I was still struggling and fighting when suddenly a terrific blast of hot air came up the shaft, and blew me right away from the air shaft and up to the surface.

"The water was now swirling round, and the ship sinking rapidly, when once again I was caught and sucked down by an inrush of water, this time adhering to one of the gratings. Just how I got clear I don't know, as I was rather losing interest in things, but I eventually came to the surface once again."

Lightoller came to the surface alongside an upside down collapsible boat. One of the *Titanic*'s huge funnels, weighing scores of tons, fell into the water just beside Lightoller, washing him, some other survivors, and the upturned lifeboat safely clear of the sinking ship. Lightoller and some thirty others survived by spending the night on the upside down boat, nearly frozen as they stood or crouched in their wet clothes in the frigid night air, until they were rescued by a ship after dawn.

Sailors who survived a series of disastrous sinkings

Lightoller was one of only 189 men in the *Titanic*'s crew who survived (686 men in the crew died). Another crew member who escaped from the *Titanic* was Frank A. Tower, a young seaman who was to survive a series of sinkings which would earn him the nickname "Lucky" Tower.

Undaunted by his escape from the *Titanic*, Tower signed on as an oiler aboard the *Empress of Ireland*, queen of the Canadian Pacific Line. On May 28, 1914, the ship left Canada for London with 1,479 on board. On its way down the St. Lawrence River during a bitterly cold night, the

Empress collided with a freighter and sank, killing 1,012 passengers and crewmen. Tower escaped on a raft, which he shared with a wealthy Toronto attorney.

When World War I began, Tower realized that he would be much safer serving on an ocean liner than in the deadly trenches of the battlefields. Therefore, he was delighted that he had become a member of the *Lusitania*'s crew. After the liner was torpedoed, Tower managed to swim away from the sinking ship. He was picked up by one of the rescue boats.

The Liverpool newspapers turned up the story that "Lucky" Tower had survived three major ship disasters and revealed the news to the public. This doomed Tower's maritime career. When he attempted to sign on another vessel, the crew—to a man—walked off. They didn't want to be on a ship with such a jinx on board. Tower tried to join the crew of another ship, and the same thing happened.

Tower finally wound up in the British Army and was sent off to fight in the trenches. Did his luck hold? That remains a mystery because, although he apparently never showed up again in his favorite pubs in Liverpool or Southampton, there was nothing to prove that he did not survive the war.

Another seaman, Casimir Polemus of Ploermel, France, also survived three shipwrecks: the loss of the *Jeanne Catherine* off Brest in 1875, the *Trois Freres*, wrecked in the Bay of Biscay in 1880, and *L'Odeon*, wrecked off Newfoundland in 1882. Fewer lives were lost than in the three shipwrecks survived by "Lucky" Tower, but the record of Polemus is extraordinary because in each shipwreck he was the only survivor.

Lost overboard

It is one thing to escape from a sinking ship or to fall overboard from a ship that is not sinking if it is known that you are in the water and need help, and if rescuers are on the way. It is entirely another story if you wind up far out in the ocean without anyone knowing about it, without a lifeboat, life jacket or life raft, and without rescuers anywhere near.

William Buie, a seventeen-year-old sailor in the U.S. Navy, had served in a destroyer for only about a month. The ex–farm boy was very seasick one night in 1959 as the ship bucked through the waves sixty miles southwest of San Diego. Buie went topside to watch a movie and then, still feeling queasy, he went aft to smoke a cigarette. As he was leaning on the side of the destroyer's deck, the ship rolled—and over, into the sea, rolled Buie.

Thrashing in the water, Buie was too shocked by the cold to shout to the stern watch. He tried to swim after the ship but soon gave up. Nobody knew that he had fallen overboard from the destroyer. As the ship's lights faded in the distance (he later said, "I guess that was about the alonest I ever felt") he quickly kicked off his shoes and blue denim dungarees. Remembering his survival training, he turned the pants into a float by knotting the legs and popping the pants sharply into the water, waistband first, to trap an air bubble in each leg.

Buie tried to keep up his spirits by singing over and over the only song he knew, "Tennessee Waltz." Soon he gave this up and began to lose hope. Then about two hours after he had fallen overboard he saw lights. It was another U.S. Navy ship sailing a random course between exercises. Buie shouted for help, and an alert sailor on watch heard him and sounded the emergency rescue alarm. The ship located him with searchlights, circled around, and a rescue swimmer dove over the side, swam to Buie, and hauled him aboard. The ship's crew, impressed by Buie's gutsy performance and great luck, figured that some of his luck might rub off on them, and invited him to join their ship.

In November 1827 a wave saved three sailors who had been washed overboard. Their eighty-ton schooner sailing from Halifax, Nova Scotia, to Bermuda with nine men and boys aboard was buffeted so violently by a storm that the mate and two sailors were washed overboard. An instant later a wave swept all three men back onto the ship unharmed.

Waves assisted in the rescue of sixteen sailors on board a grounded freighter, which was breaking up in very heavy seas off the coast of England in 1941. The imperiled seamen had tied themselves to the funnel, but a rescue boat couldn't reach them because the crew couldn't safely pull it alongside the freighter. Finally Henry Blogg, coxswain of the rescue craft, carefully gauged a huge wave and the boat rode it onto the deck of the grounded ship. After the freighter's crew climbed into the rescue boat, Blogg used another wave to launch his boat back into the sea, accomplishing the unusual rescue without the loss of a single life.

In 1923 a French trader, Adolphe Pons, and his native assistant were cruising along in a motor launch eight miles off the coast of New Caledonia when Pons suddenly fell overboard. Without thinking, the native dived overboard to assist Pons, leaving the motorboat heading away from the two men under full power with no one aboard. The men were in a terrible situation since they were so far out to sea, in water filled with sharks. However, soon they saw that the motorboat was turning by itself, circling back to them so that they were able to climb aboard to safety.

An assorted variety of objects have saved people washed overboard who managed to climb onto them and float to safety. In 1834 two Maori women, the only survivors from a sunken canoe in Cook Strait off New Zealand, were left swimming far at sea and in great danger of drowning. They saved their own lives when they came across the floating carcass of a dead whale with the harpoon still stuck in it. The women used a line trailing from the harpoon to pull themselves aboard the carcass and floated more than eighty miles to safety.

In 1872 the U.S. *Polaris* was crushed by ice in the arctic. Nineteen sailors from the ship climbed aboard an iceberg and drifted for 196 days—a total distance of twelve hundred miles—until they were rescued from their chilly raft off the coast of Labrador.

In 1931 three aviators—Willi Rody and two companions—were attempting to fly nonstop from Lisbon, Portugal, to New York when they ran out of fuel and ditched at sea, ninety-two miles off Cape Race, Newfoundland. Rody, only twenty-one years old, had bought the plane with part of his inheritance and named it the *Esa*, after his new bride. The plane had no radio to send requests for help, and since the aircraft was not a seaplane they could expect to be swimming very soon far out in the ocean after the plane sank. They would die within a short time in the frigid water. It is rare for a land plane to stay afloat for more than four or five minutes after ditching—many have gone down less than two minutes after landing in the water —and often all aboard are lost, trapped in the crunched, broken fuselage.

The plane continued to float for hours, however, and the three fliers spent the first night standing in the cockpit with their legs in water, expecting the plane to sink at any time. When the aircraft was still afloat the next morning, they crawled out on a wing to watch for ships. They had only seven ounces of mushy chocolate for food, and they rationed water from the engine to drink, a sip at a time.

The castaways sat on the plane for six seemingly endless days, weakened by hunger and constant soaking in the icy water. Finally they spotted a passing ship and frantically waved a flag, but the ship's crew didn't see them and continued on its way. Then, on the seventh day after the crash, they attracted the attention of a passing Norwegian freighter headed for Russia and were rescued—after spending a week on a plane that had no right to float at all. The Norwegian freighter transferred the three men to an American ship bound for New York, and the American vessel steered past the location where they had abandoned the plane. No airplane was there to be seen—it had sunk shortly after their rescue.

133 days alone on a life raft

There are many cases of lengthy survivals in small open boats or in life rafts, but the record for a sea survivor was set by Poon Lim, a Chinese seaman, who floated alone on his life raft in the south Atlantic for 133 days.

The twenty-five-year-old sailor had left his native Hainan Island (off the south coast of China) to join the crew of a British merchant ship during World War II. The ship left Capetown with a crew of fifty-five in November 1942, but it was torpedoed by a German submarine when it was well out in the Atlantic Ocean. Poon Lim jumped over the side of the sinking ship wearing a life jacket and began to look for a life raft. He saw one with five sailors on it, but it drifted away from him (those five sailors were to be the only other survivors of the ship).

After struggling in the water for two hours, Poon Lim saw an unoccupied life raft several hundred feet away and swam to it. The emergency raft had been made of timbers and was eight feet in both length and width. Tied to it were a large jug of water, some tins of biscuits, several flares, and an electric torch.

Poon Lim figured that if he limited himself to a small ration of water and biscuits each day he would be able to stay alive for at least a month. As time passed, Poon Lim saw potential rescuers several times—a freighter went by at close range, a U.S. Navy plane flew overhead, and a German submarine appeared near him—but each time no rescue came. He realized that he would have to do everything possible to stay alive for a long time on the raft.

He used the canvas covering of the life jacket as a receptacle to collect rainwater. He took apart the electric torch and removed a wire which he made into a fish hook. It took him days to shape the metal into a hook, using the water jug for a hammer. He used the rope which had been used to tie down supplies on the raft for a fishing line.

Finally, Poon Lim baited the hook with a biscuit, tossed the fishing line into the sea, and waited for a bite. When he managed to hook a fish and pull it in, he used the edge of the biscuit tin to cut the fish in half. Poon Lim ate the raw flesh and used what remained of the fish as bait to catch another fish.

One day Poon Lim saw some seagulls and made plans

to catch one. He gathered seaweed that was stuck to the bottom of the raft and molded it into a form which resembled a bird's nest. He put pieces of fish by the "nest" and lay still, waiting for a gull to land. A bird landed to grab the fish and Poon Lim managed to catch it despite suffering deep cuts from its claws and beak. To carve up his new dinner he fashioned a knife. First, he pried up a nail from the raft's planking. Then, he used the nail to tear a piece of metal from the empty ration tin. Finally, he pounded the metal into the form of a knife by using his shoe as a hammer.

Poon Lim used the remains of the next bird he caught as bait to hook a shark. He braided his fishing line to make it stronger, wrapped his hands in canvas from the life jacket to protect them from injury while struggling with the shark, and after he had pulled the shark aboard, finished it off by using the water jug half filled with sea water as a weapon. He ate a huge meal from the shark and then sliced its fins and let them dry in the sun, a Hainan delicacy.

To keep his body in good condition, Poon Lim exercised twice a day by swimming around the raft, always keeping his head above water to watch for sharks. He counted the passing days by marking notches on the side of the raft.

On the morning of the 133rd day, Poon Lim saw a boat. Because his flares were gone he signaled by stripping off his shirt and waving it frantically. He was picked up by three Brazilians who gave him water and beans and took him to Belem, at the mouth of the Amazon River in Brazil. He had floated clear across the Atlantic.

Poon Lim walked ashore unaided. He had lost twenty pounds, but after spending four weeks in a Brazilian hospital he was pronounced fit and released. Poon Lim had become famous, and his tremendous efforts to stay alive won him many honors. King George VI personally awarded him the British Empire Medal, the highest British civilian award. The British Navy had booklets printed which described his survival techniques and placed them in all life rafts. Senator Warren Magnuson introduced a bill, which was passed by the U.S. Senate and the House of Representatives, allowing Poon Lim to become a permanent resident of the United States.

Unusual survival of a ship collision

In contrast to Poon Lim, fourteen-year-old Linda Morgan had the fastest escape to safety on record after her ship began to sink. In 1956 the *Andrea Doria*, an Italian liner, collided with the Swedish-American Line's *Stockholm*. A sailor on the deck of the *Stockholm* was knocked down by the impact, got up in time to see the *Andrea Doria* veering away, and then heard a voice calling for her mother.

The girl was pulled from wreckage on the *Stockholm*'s bow by three sailors and carried by one of the men toward the ship's hospital. They were intercepted by the ship's chief purser who asked the girl for her name. "Linda Morgan," she replied. "Where's my mother? Do you know where my mother is?" "No," the man replied, "but I'll look for her." The chief purser was puzzled to see that neither the name of Linda Morgan or her mother were in the ship's passenger list. Finally Linda, becoming aware that her surroundings looked unfamiliar, said, "I was on the *Andrea Doria*. Where am I now?"

Linda Morgan wound up on the *Stockholm*, because the *Stockholm*'s bow had smashed through the side of the *Andrea Doria*, swooped beneath her bed in cabin fifty-two on the *Andrea Doria*, then carried her away to safety as the two ships separated. She had landed behind a curved sea breaker wall, two-and-one-half feet high, on the *Stockholm*'s bow. This wall, designed to prevent sea waves breaking over the ship's bow from reaching electrical equipment, had shielded the girl from flying fragments of wreckage.

Linda's sister, sleeping in the same cabin, had been crushed to death by the *Stockholm*'s reinforced icebreaker bow, which had plunged thirty feet into the side of the Andrea Doria. It shattered the watertight compartments, punctured a fuel tank, and knocked out the generator.

When the *Stockholm* pulled back from the *Andrea Doria* her bow was smashed but the ship could still float. The *Andrea Doria*, however, was doomed. Rescue ships saved 1,650 people from the sinking liner, but fifty-one people died in the collision.

CHAPTER 13

Avalanche Adventures

O*ne brilliant* morning in California's Yosemite Valley after a heavy snow fall, John Muir decided to climb by a side canyon to the top of a ridge a little over three thousand feet above the canyon floor. There he planned to view the frequent avalanches that occurred above the valley after a snowstorm and also see broad views of the whitened forest and summit peaks. Muir had estimated that he could reach the top of the ridge in three or four hours, but the loose snow made the climb more difficult than he had anticipated. Within a half hour or so of sunset he was still several hundred feet from the summit.

As Muir struggled in the snow near the canyon head, most of the time sinking at least waist deep, he suddenly started an avalanche and began to shoot down the slope along with the violent rush of snow.

"When the avalanche started I threw myself on my back and spread my arms to keep from sinking. Fortunately, though the grade of the canyon is very steep, it is not interrupted by precipices large enough to cause outbounding or free plunging. On no part of the rush was I buried. I was only moderately imbedded on the surface or at times a little below it, and covered with a veil of back-streaming dust particles. As the whole mass beneath and about me joined in the flight, there was no friction, though I was tossed here and there and lurched from side to side. When the avalanche came to rest I found myself on top of the crumpled pile without a bruise or scar. This was a fine experience. Hawthorne says somewhere that steam has spiritualized travel; though unspiritual smells, smoke, etc., still attend steam travel. This flight, in what might be called a milky way of snow stars, was the most spiritual and exhilarating of all the modes of motion that I have ever experienced. Elijah's flight in a chariot of fire would hardly have been more gloriously exciting."

It had taken John Muir nearly all day to climb close to the top of the ridge, but the descent took only about a minute. He enjoyed his perilous ride because, "The start was so sudden and the end came so soon I had but little time to think of the danger that attends this sort of travel, though at such times one thinks fast."

In 1932, two climbers had a wild avalanche ride of about 2,250 feet down a steep slope near Chamonix in eastern France. An expert alpine climber named Greloz and a strong but less experienced climber named Vallvet were climbing a sheer cliff when a small avalanche poured over them. They succeeded in hanging on to the cliff and decided to continue their climb.

As the two men neared the top, a bigger avalanche roared down toward them. Greloz, roped to Vallvet and climbing above him, had his body pushed away from the cliff as the snow rushed between him and the slope. He lost his grip, fell past Vallvet in a cloud of snow dust, and the jerk on the rope pulled Vallvet off the cliff.

As the climbers fell with the avalanche they began to leapfrog, first one man and then the other in front, bouncing like two rag dolls. At each bounce they lost more equipment—hats, scarves, glasses, crampons, gloves, etc. The fall seemed endless to them, and as they bounced down the slope they kept expecting that the next bump would kill them.

The two men finally came to a stop on more level terrain. Neither had been seriously injured by the fall although both were cut and bruised. Their gyrations during the fall had so knotted the climbing rope that its original length of thirty three feet had been reduced to five feet.

Phillip Gosset vividly described an avalanche ride that he experienced while climbing above the Rhone Valley in 1864 with a friend and several guides.

"The ground on which we were standing began to move slowly. I soon sank up to my shoulders and began descending backward. The speed of the avalanche increased rapidly and before long I was covered up with snow. I was suffocating when I suddenly came to the surface again. I was on a wave of the avalanche and saw it before me as I was carried down. It was the most awful sight I ever saw. The head of the avalanche was already at the spot where we had made our last halt. The head was preceded by a thick cloud of snow dust; the rest of the avalanche was clear. Around me I heard the horrid hissing of the snow and far below me the thundering of the foremost part of the avalanche.

"To prevent myself sinking again I made use of my arms in much the same manner as when swimming in a standing position. Then I saw the pieces of snow in front of me stop at some yards distance; then the snow straight before me stopped and I heard on a grand scale the same creaking sound that is made by a heavy cart passing over frozen snow in winter. I instantly threw up both arms to protect my head in case I should again be covered up. I had stopped, but the snow behind me was still in motion; its pressure on my body was so strong that I thought I should be crushed to death. I was covered up by the snow coming down behind me. My first impulse was to try to uncover my head, but this I could not do for the avalanche had frozen by pressure the moment it stopped, and I was frozen in."

Gosset was very lucky because his hands were sticking above the surface. One of the guides, who had been able to free himself, quickly uncovered Gosset's head. Gosset couldn't crawl free until he was cut loose with an ice axe.

Gosset's friend was buried with his feet sticking out but was already dead when released. The body of one of the guides was dug out of the snow three days later from beneath eight feet of snow.

A lifesaving avalanche

In 1980 an avalanche on Canada's highest mountain, Mount Logan, probably saved the lives of two falling mountain climbers. Peter Perren and Tim Auger, both Banff National Park wardens, slipped and began to plummet down sheer ice cliffs toward a glacier, almost two thousand feet below. When the men fell they started an avalanche which immediately swallowed them up. The falling torrent of snow cushioned them from impacts on the mountainside and on the glacier itself. When they landed on an avalanche fan atop the glacier, Auger was buried in snow but still roped to Perren. Perren dug him out, and four hours later a helicopter called by rescuers picked them up and flew them to a hospital. Auger had a cracked shoulder blade and a chipped backbone and Perren had a severely dislocated knee, but without the avalanche to cushion their fall they would most likely not have been alive at all.

In contrast to those few who have survived rides on avalanches, most caught in an avalanche face a good chance of either a quick or slow death. They can die instantly if they are hurled against obstacles such as trees or if they are struck by rocks or other debris carried within the avalanche.

Avalanche burials

Buried victims may die more slowly by suffocation if they have inhaled snow which blocks air passages, if the pressure of overlying snow prevents them from expanding their lungs, or if they simply use up the surrounding oxygen. The snow around the face of someone buried by an avalanche may melt, due to the warmth of body heat and exhaled air, and then freeze again, forming an ice mask over the face that seals off any source of air.

Imprisonment in an avalanche often feels similar to being encased in concrete. It may be impossible to move as much as a finger. Unless one has an air pocket to supply oxygen or is dug out in a short time, there is little chance of survival.

Once in an avalanche, the best thing to do is to keep your mouth clamped shut (to avoid inhaling powder snow) and make strong swimming motions with your arms and legs to stay on the surface. When the avalanche slows down, you should move an arm in front of your nose and mouth so that you will have a breathing space if you become completely buried. If you are buried you should make just one strong effort to free yourself by thrusting upward. If your initial attempt to break out fails, you should lie still, calm yourself, and hope for a prompt rescue. Further exertions or just fear itself will result in the use of far more oxygen.

People who fear being buried by an avalanche can take some safety precautions. The simplest is to wear an avalanche cord—a red cord about thirty yards long and a quarter inch in diameter that is tied around the waist and then worn like a long tail. If you are buried by an avalanche, some of the cord should remain on the surface and the rescuers can pull it up until it goes down vertically and then dig you out. Climbers wearing avalanche cords, while much safer, do have a comical appearance. One observer described it this way: "The vision of a line of sturdy mountaineers tripping intricately across a snowfield like embarrassed macaws in pursuit of each other's scarlet tails may give us some pleasureable moments." For those who don't want to walk or ski dragging a long cord behind them, there are also electronic devices that can be worn so that if someone is buried, rescuers can quickly locate the victim by where the signal is strongest on their own monitors.

The number of victims who have been killed by burial in some huge avalanches is staggering. In 1970, 20,000 people died when avalanches covered a city in the Peruvian Andes. During World War I, at least forty thousand soldiers were killed by avalanches as the Austrian and Italian armies battled for control of mountain regions. Some of these avalanches were natural, but many were caused by the armies themselves, as soldiers shelled the snowfields above enemy troops to start slides. Whether man-made or natural, avalanches justify the saying that "Snow is not a wolf in sheep's clothing, it is a tiger in lamb's clothing."

Another nightmarish aspect of avalanche burial is that sound travels well when going down through snow, but very little sound from below passes up to the surface. For example, ski patrolmen purposely buried beneath two feet of snow to help train dogs to find avalanche victims reported that they clearly heard the dogs' paws walking on the snow, but when they shouted upward, not a sound was heard above.

Although victims of avalanche burial are usually tightly entombed, avalanche snow can, on rare occasions, be quite loose. In 1953 a forestry worker was buried in a vertical position, in loose and porous snow. He struggled until he freed his hands, and then by digging with his hands and twisting and turning his body and legs he managed to gain freedom of movement. He began to pull snow from above his head, passed it down his body, and then stood on it— thereby raising himself slowly, step-by-step, up through the snow. After an hour and a half of excruciating effort, he pulled himself up out of the hole, totally exhausted.

In 1668 a young man buried by an avalanche at St. Antonien, a remote village near the Swiss-Austrian border, was saved by the action of a river. Conrad Ladner was cutting a hole in the river ice when an avalanche slammed into him, burying him on the far bank and damming the river. Gradually the river undermined the snow mass in its center until it collapsed. A crack then opened on each bank, one of them directly over Ladner. He crawled out, unharmed, from a depth of seven feet.

In general, the more a buried victim's body is free of contact with snow and the larger their airspace, the longer he can survive under the snow. In cases where people are completely surrounded by snow, the odds are great against surviving for more than half an hour. However, there have been some rare exceptions.

On a Sunday afternoon in January 1945, a twenty-one-year-old Swiss farmer's daughter set out to visit her fiancé in a neighboring village. She was crossing a gully when she was suddenly buried by a small avalanche and completely enveloped in snow. She was not found until the next morning when rescuers probed the avalanche, knowing that her route had to cross the gully.

Nobody expected to find her alive since it had been twenty-one hours since she had first been buried. The rescuers were amazed when they found her and the "corpse" opened its eyes and spoke to them. Although she was stiff and had slight frostbite of her hands and feet, she recovered fully, married, and became the mother of a large family.

How had the girl survived for twenty-one hours, completely surrounded by snow? She had been in a shallow avalanche so she was probably near enough to the surface to get a limited supply of oxygen. She was dressed in warm clothes which kept her temperature from dropping too low, but some cooling of her body could have been very helpful. As we discovered in the case of Armando Socarras, who survived a nine-hour flight at thirty thousand feet in the landing gear well of a jetliner at temperatures as low as forty degrees below zero Fahrenheit (Chapter eight), a lowered body temperature slows down metabolism and reduces the need for oxygen. As the girl lay in a light coma, her cooled body could survive with the limited oxygen supply.

As body temperatures fall far below normal (much lower than the Swiss farm girl's temperature must have been), oxygen use declines dramatically. At a body temperature of ninety-two degrees Fahrenheit, oxygen consumption is eighty percent of normal; at eighty-six degrees Fahrenheit, it is seventy percent of normal; and at seventy-four degrees Fahrenheit, it is only fifty percent of normal.

How cold can a person become and still recover? In February 1951, doctors were stunned to see an indication of how great a loss of body temperature can be survived. Dorothy Mae Stevens of Chicago had passed out from drinking and slept unprotected all night in a Chicago alley in temperatures that fell to eleven degrees below zero. Her body temperature had dropped to 60.8 degrees Fahrenheit, her pulse rate was barely twelve beats per minute, her breaths came three times a minute, and she had no measurable blood pressure. Doctors didn't expect her to survive, but they administered cortisone and swaddled her arms and legs in gauze to keep the flesh from chipping off. Within twenty-four hours, Mrs. Stevens was conscious and taking liquid nourishment. A week later she was eating solid food and had a temperature of 100.2 degrees. She lost both legs and all but one finger to amputations, but six months later she left the hospital and lived until 1974.

The limited oxygen requirements at low body temperatures are most dramatically shown when apparent drowning victims are sometimes revived after spending long periods of time submerged in icy water. In February 1974 Vegard Slettmoen, aged five, fell through the ice on a Norwegian river. He was discovered forty minutes later, eight feet below the surface, but was revived in a hospital and suffered no brain damage. How could anyone survive what would seem to be such a fatally long time under chilling water? Vegard was saved by a phenomenon known as the diving reflex, which can be triggered after humans fall into water colder than seventy degrees Fahrenheit. The reflex causes the windpipe to close, preventing water from entering the lungs. After being submerged in the freezing water, the body's functions slow down and much smaller amounts of oxygen are needed to maintain life.

Getting back to avalanches, let's look at how long some avalanche burial victims have survived when they were not totally enveloped in snow. In 1951 Gerhard Freissegger, a young Austrian, was buried for twelve and a half days, after an avalanche smashed into the three-room hut where he was staying while working on a dam construction project. When the snow hit him he was in his bunk wearing only a shirt and underpants. His legs and left arm were completely immobilized by snow, and he had only a small air space over his face and chest, kept clear of snow by a roof timber. His right hand was the only part of his body which he could move to any extent. He could hear rescuers walking about above, talking, shoveling, and probing as they searched for bodies, but his own shouts for help were unheard. Even though the men were close by for three days, and once a probe hit a timber right next to Freissegger, the rescuers didn't find him.

By the fourth day, the snow covering Freissegger began to melt so that his left arm and his legs down to his knees were free. He cleared the snow away from his upper body and began to dig with his hands at the hard snow above him. He made little progress because his lower legs were still trapped in the snow and this limited his range of movement. Freissegger finally managed to free his severely frostbitten legs on the eighth day after being trapped. He used a splinter of wood to bore upwards through the snow, eating large amounts of snow to assuage his terrible thirst.

Freissegger finally noticed a faint patch of light above him on about the tenth day. He widened the hole, poked his head out, and saw that dusk was falling. He shouted weakly for help and then sunk back into his hole. He knew that if he crawled out, wearing only a shirt and undershorts, he would freeze to death in the frigid night air.

After twelve and a half days of entrapment, Freissegger heard voices, shouted for help, and was rescued. He had lost about sixty five pounds, and both of his legs had to be amputated below the knee. Months later he returned to work, walking on artificial legs.

Freissegger could never have survived so long in the

avalanche if he had not been partly free of snow. The air space over his face and chest and a fierce will to live were the main factors that allowed him to escape death.

Thirty-seven days under the snow

Even longer cases of survival under an avalanche have taken place where victims were not in contact with snow. In 1755 Maria Anna Rochia, her sister-in-law, her thirteen-year-old daughter, and her six-year-old son were trapped with the livestock in stables behind their home when an avalanche covered their farm in the Stura Valley of Italy with fifty feet of snow. The men of the family had been away at the time of the avalanche. When they returned, they assumed that no one could be alive beneath all that snow and made no rescue attempts.

But the women and children were alive. The snow's weight had caved in the stables' roof so the four were trapped in a space twelve feet long, eight feet wide, and five feet high. All the livestock died within the first few days except for two goats, one with milk and the other about to kid. Maria Anna's sister-in-law had fifteen chestnuts in her pocket, and when these were gone they had only one quart a day of goat milk to feed all four of them.

The boy died on about the twelfth day after suffering violent stomach pains, but the two women and the girl survived for thirty-seven days under the snow. After the kid was born, the women killed it, ate the meat raw, and drank the extra milk of the mother goat. The three imprisoned Italians were nearly driven out of their minds during the ordeal by the odors of the decaying bodies and the constant drip of melted snow water.

When the spring thaw uncovered the top of the shed, the men returned to recover and bury the bodies of their family. Instead, they got the shock of their lives when they found the two women and the girl alive. It was many weeks before Maria Anna Rochia was able to walk again, but her sister-in-law and daughter recovered much more quickly.

The disappearing avalanche

Some very lucky people have been saved from avalanches when apparently unstoppable torrents of snow were diverted at the last second. In 1952 James Riddell and a party of climbers were tramping up a Swiss peak on skis when they heard a loud crack and saw a wave of snow and ice blocks plunging down toward them. The wave was at least one hundred feet high, and the men had no chance of escape, so they merely turned their backs toward the approaching avalanche. A cloud of snow particles darkened the sky, the roar of the avalanche grew ever louder, and they expected to be crushed by the smothering ice and snow. To their amazement the roar subsided and then they heard only silence. They turned and saw that an enormous crevasse had appeared where previously there had been none. A snow bridge over the crevasse had collapsed under the weight of the avalanche, and the part of the huge falling mass of ice and snow that was directed at them disappeared down into the earth.

Has anyone who has been buried by an avalanche ever been saved by being uncovered by a second avalanche? In 1689 an avalanche buried three hundred people in the Montafon Valley of Switzerland. A priest was on his way to give sacrament to the victims when he was buried by one avalanche and promptly uncovered by a second avalanche which carried the snow above him on down the mountain.

CHAPTER 14

Surviving Earthquakes, Volcanoes, and Forest Fires

*I*n *August* 1868, the USS *Wateree*, a Civil War, side-wheeler, flat-bottomed gunboat, was stationed at Arica, Peru (now Arica is in North Chile). The boat's flat bottom was to prove her salvation when a powerful earthquake sent a huge seismic sea wave crashing into the *Wateree* and other ships anchored off Arica. Rear Adm. L. G. Billings, who was on board at the time, gave a vivid account of the incident.

"We were startled by a terrific noise on shore, as of a tremendous roar of musketry, lasting several minutes. Again the trembling earth waved to and fro, and this time the sea receded until the shipping was left stranded, while as far to seaward as our vision could reach we saw the rocky bottom of the sea, never before exposed to human gaze, with struggling fish and monsters of the deep left high and dry.

"The round-bottomed ships keeled over on their beam ends, while the *Wateree* rested easily on her floorlike bottom; and when the returning sea, not like a wave, but rather like an enormous tide, came sweeping back, rolling our unfortunate companion ships over and over, leaving some bottom up and others masses of wreckage, the *Wateree* rose easily over the tossing waters unharmed."

The wave, with a maximum height of seventy feet, then carried the *Wateree* far inland.

This passage and its outcome were described by another witness. The *Wateree* was "carried by an exceptionally heavy wave completely over the town, scraping the tops of the highest buildings, and was safely deposited on some sandy wasteland about a mile inland. Thanks to her flat bottom she fetched up on an even keel, and although it was impossible to get the ship back to her accustomed element she was in no danger structurally. The ship was therefore left in full commission for several months until sold. Service routine continued, but with certain readjustments. Sanitary facilities were erected ashore and a vegetable garden was started. The most unusual modification was the substitution of burros for boats. If the captain wanted to go 'ashore,' the bosun's mate would pipe and call, 'Away brig.' Thereupon the coxswain would run out on a boom, slide down a pennant to a burro, cast off, and come alongside to the ladder, which had been lengthened to reach the ground. The captain would mount and ride off into the dunes."

The crew found nearby the wreck of another ship, with her anchor chains wound around her as many times as they would go, indicating that she had been rolled over and over by the force of the water. Had the *Wateree* not been a flat-bottomed ship she would undoubtedly have suffered the same fate.

In 1958 an even larger earthquake-caused wave carried two boats to great heights over land-based obstacles in Alaska. Howard Ulrich, a commercial fisherman, and his seven-year-old son were anchored in Alaska's Lituya Bay in his thirty-eight-foot fishing boat, *Edrie*. Two other fishing boats, the *Badger* and the *Sunmore*, were anchored closer to the bay's entrance, just inside a sand spit that extends across a good part of the bay's mouth. On the night of July 9 at 10:17 P.M. (when it was still light in this far north latitude) a violent earthquake struck, churning the water and causing huge masses of ice and snow to fall off cliffs around the steep-sided bay.

As Ulrich stared awestruck, he saw thousands of tons of

earth, rock, and ice plunge into the bay, splashing up a huge wave that exploded across the bay at enormous height. The wave was about one hundred feet high, stretching two-and-a-half miles from one shore to another, and it was headed toward Ulrich and his son at what was later to be estimated as 130 mph.

Ulrich tried to haul up the anchor so he could get to deep water before the wave threw the boat up against the rocks on the side of the bay, but for some reason the anchor was stuck on the bottom. Desperately Ulrich let the anchor chain pay out to its full 240-foot length in the hope that there would be enough slack to allow his boat to ride up over the wave. Then with engine and rudder he began to maneuver the boat so that it would face into the oncoming wall of water.

Ulrich had not quite swung the boat's bow into the wave when it hit. "It was like going up in an elevator," he said. "Only there seemed to be no end to it. The half-inch anchor chain snapped off at the winch like a piece of kite string, and the short end came snapping back around the pilothouse and almost took my head off."

The wave, carrying along Ulrich's boat, washed up the mountain on the opposite side from the ice and rockfall, scouring the rocky face clear of vegetation to a height of 1,750 feet. The fishing boat swooped along high above the treetops as it rode the wave up the mountainside. "There was just nothing I could do," Ulrich said. "I could see the trees snapping off way below us. I figured we had to be dumped and smashed on the rocks."

The fishing boat was saved by a great stroke of luck when it slid back over the wave's crest and was caught by the backwash of water returning down to the bay. Ulrich threw his throttle wide open and frantically tried to keep the bow aimed toward the bay. When the backwash had carried him down the mountainside, back into the bay, Ulrich marveled to see the shoreside slopes, thick with timber only moments before, now naked, shorn to glistening rock to a height of as much as 1,750 feet. In the bay, felled trees were pitching and tossing in the churning water and great chunks of glacier ice spun round and round, grinding against one another. Despite all the floating obstacles, Ulrich was able to carefully thread his way through the bay and out its mouth into the open sea.

The other two fishing boats, the *Badger* and the *Sunmore*, had also been caught by overpowering waves. The fifty-five-foot *Sunmore* was swept against a cliff, and no trace of it or its crew was ever found. The *Badger* was carried by the wave sweeping toward the ocean clear over the 150-yard-wide spit of rock at the mouth of the bay and out into the open sea. The *Badger*'s captain, Bill Swanson, reported that, "I looked down on rocks as big as houses when we crossed the spit." The *Badger* smashed into the ocean surface, stern-first, a quarter of a mile offshore. The boat began to sink and Swanson and his wife, Vivian, floated away in their eight-foot lifeboat. Two hours later, shivering and shocked, they were rescued by another fishing boat.

Port Royal, Jamaica, a thriving city of eight thousand that was sometimes called the "Wickedest City in the World," was destroyed by a violent earthquake and a subsequent seismic sea wave in 1692. Almost two-thirds of the wharf area slid into the sea when the first shocks hit, collapsing eighteen hundred houses and killing approximately two thousand people. The harbor waters withdrew and then roared back to shore, flooding streets and houses and killing hundreds more. Many ships anchored in the harbor were sunk, but the HMS *Swan*, a British ship in drydock for scraping and repairing of its hull, was washed over the dock area into the central part of the city. There, the *Swan* picked up numerous survivors, who were struggling in the flood waters. Following the earthquake and flooding, another one thousand inhabitants died of disease and injuries, and the city was abandoned forever. However, many of the two or three story homes under twenty to forty feet of water remained visible under the sea for the next hundred years.

Many people in earthquakes have survived in falling buildings—such as the extraordinary case of a newborn infant who survived a burial of six days in hospital rubble after the September 1985 Mexico City earthquake—but one of the most unique cases of victims surviving a falling building took place in Niigata, Japan, in 1964. When the earthquake struck Niigata, an apartment block survived the shaking but began to sink with an alarming tilt as liquefaction undermined the ground beneath it. (Powerful shaking can change water-saturated granular material from a solid to a liquid state.) The multistoried apartment building finally came to rest at an angle eighty degrees off the vertical. The amazed inhabitants on the top floors climbed out of their windows and walked down the gently sloping side of the building to the street.

A whimsical account of an earthquake survival took place after the flamboyant actor John Barrymore experienced the San Francisco earthquake of 1906. Barrymore immediately sent a telegram to his sister Ethel, describing as dramatically as possible—in the thirty words allotted to him—how he had been thrown out of bed and had wandered in a daze to the street, where an army sergeant gave him a shovel and made him work for twenty-four hours among the ruins of the city.

Ethel showed the exaggerated account to their uncle, John Drew and asked him if he believed it. Drew replied, "Every word. It took an act of God to get him out of bed, and the United States Army to put him to work."

A walk on the rim of an erupting volcano

Volcanoes have also been associated with some notable survival stories. Haroun Tazieff, a geologist, adventurer, photographer, and author, once wandered to the very edge of an erupting volcano and lived to give a singular account of what he saw and experienced.

"I am now almost directly over the roaring chasm, and my gaze goes straight down into it like a stone dropping into a pit. After all, it's nothing but a tunnel. That's all. It's a vertical tunnel, ten or fifteen yards across, its walls heated to such a degree that they stretch and 'rise' like dough. Up from its depths every now and then enormous drops of liquid fire spurt forth, a great splashing sweat that falls and vanishes, golden flash upon flash, back into the dazzling gulf. Even the brownish vapors emanating from the pit cannot quite veil its splendor. It is nothing but a tunnel running down into viscous copper-colored draperies; yet it opens into the very substance of another world. The sight is so extraordinary that I forget the insecurity of my position and the hellish burning under the soles of my feet. Quite mechanically, I go on lifting first the left foot, then the right. It is as though my mind were held fast in a trap by the sight of this burning well from which a terrifying snore continually rises, interrupted by sharp explosions and the rolling of thunder.

"Suddenly I hurl myself backward; the flight of projectives [volcanic bombs consisting of molten lava] has whizzed past my face. Hunched up again, instinctively trying to make as small a target of myself as I can [to avoid being hit by the bombs as they crash back to earth], I am in the thick of this hairsbreadth game of anticipation and dodging.

"And now it's all over; I take a last glance into the marvelous and terrible abyss, and am just getting ready to start off on the last stage of this circumnavigation, all two hundred yards of it, when I get a sudden sharp blow in the back. A delayed-action bomb! With all the breath knocked out of me, I stand rigid.

"A moment passes. I wonder why I am not dead. But nothing seems to have happened to me—no pain, no change of any sort. Slowly I risk turning my head, and at my feet I see a sort of huge red loaf with all the glow dying out of it.

"I stretch my arms and wriggle my back. Nothing hurts. Everything seems to be in its proper place. Later on, examining my jacket, I discovered a brownish scorch mark with slightly charred edges, about the size of my hand, and I drew from it a conclusion of immense value to me in future explorations: so long as one is not straight in the line of fire, volcanic bombs, which fall in a still-pasty state, but already covered with a kind of very thin elastic skin, graze one without having time to cause a deep burn."

The most extraordinary volcano survivals

One of the most terrible of all volcanic disasters was the explosion of Mt. Pelee on the island of Martinique in 1902. Enormous gas pressure built up beneath the cone, which finally exploded with an ear-splitting roar. A huge black cloud, laced with lightning, shot straight up into the sky, and a second cloud, lighter gray and traced through with red glowing lines, rolled with hurricane force down the slope of the mountain, clinging close to the ground and flattening trees in its path. The cloud, made up of steam estimated at fifteen hundred degrees Fahrenheit mixed with other gases and cinders and ashes, headed at one hundred miles per hour straight for St. Pierre, a bustling seaport on Martinique known as the "Paris of the Antilles." The picturesque city, "a sprightly mixture of French sophistication and Caribbean exuberance, sporting fashionable shops, outdoor cafes, an opera house, and a magnificent cathedral,"* instantly burst into flame as the cloud of hellfire engulfed it. One inhalation of the superheated steam was enough to kill anyone who breathed it. Others, on the edge of the cloud or protected by still air in closed rooms, felt their skin becoming unbearably hot. Some ran, some dropped to their knees to pray, and others closed windows and doors, but they died too. Within three minutes, more than thirty thousand people in St. Pierre were dead, and only two very lucky inhabitants were still alive.

Leon Comprere-Leandre, a twenty-eight-year-old shoemaker had survived. "I was seated on the doorstep of my house, which was in the southeastern part of the city. . . . All of a sudden I felt a terrible wind blowing, the earth began to tremble, and the sky suddenly became dark. I turned to go into the house, made with great difficulty the three or four steps that separated me from my room, and felt my arms and legs burning, also my body; I dropped upon a table. At this moment four others sought refuge in my room, crying and writhing in pain, although their gar-

*James Cornell, *The Great International Disaster Book* (New York: Pocket Books, 1979), 222.

ments showed no signs of having been touched by flame. At the end of ten minutes, one of those, the young Delavand girl, aged about ten years, fell dead; the others left. I then got up and went into another room, where I found the father Delavand, still clothed and lying on the bed, dead. He was purple and inflated, but the clothing was intact. I went out and found in the court two corpses interlocked: they were the bodies of the two young men who had before been with me in the room. Crazed and almost overcome, I threw myself upon a bed, inert and awaiting death. My sense returned to me in perhaps an hour, when I beheld the roof burning. With sufficient strength left, my legs bleeding and covered with burns, I ran to Fonds-Saint-Denis (the island's capital), six kilometers from St. Pierre. With the exception of the persons of whom I have spoken, I heard no human cries . . . the entire city was aflame."

Scores of villages and plantations along the outskirts of St. Pierre were also destroyed, along with all but one of the eighteen ships in the harbor. An estimated two hundred sailors on the ships were killed.

When rescuers reached the ruined town, at first they found no one still alive. However, three days after the disaster, a few searchers were walking over the ash-covered ground near the main buildings of the town when they heard a faint cry for help. "Where are you?" they shouted. The cries for help seemed to come from beneath their feet. The voice replied, "I'm down here in the dungeon of the jail. Help! Save me! Get me out!"

The rescuers removed debris until they uncovered the steps leading below ground level to the dungeon. In a small, windowless cell they found the second survivor of the catastrophe, Auguste Ciparis. As he had been waiting for his breakfast on the morning of the eruption, hot ash-filled air poured into his room through the narrow door-grating on the side of the building away from the volcano. He called for help, but no one came. The fierce heat that scorched him lasted only for a minute. None of his clothing caught fire, but his back and legs were severely burned by hot air and ash. His cell was half-filled with rubble from the prison block which had collapsed on top of it. As he sat for three days among the debris he had no food, but he did have drinking water.

Auguste Ciparis and Leon Comprere-Leandre both recovered from their burns and were able to profit from their extraordinary survivals. Ciparis was pardoned and gained fame in the Barnum and Bailey Circus and various carnival sideshows as "the Prisoner of St. Pierre." Until his death in 1929, he earned his living by appearing before the public, locked during show hours in a replica of his prison cell. Comprere-Leandre was hired to be a caretaker and special constable in St. Pierre, guiding tourists through the ruins of the town. He lived until 1936.

Staying alive in the worst forest fire in American history

Forest fires have sometimes produced such enormous heat that their effects have been almost as bad as what happened in St. Pierre. On a night in October 1871, the worst forest fire in American history started near Peshtigo, Wisconsin, a town of two thousand people centered around the lumber industry. The inhabitants first heard a low rumbling noise, and as the roaring sound and air temperature increased alarmingly, a huge tongue of flame suddenly shot over trees to the west of town. Ten minutes later, the town was engulfed in an explosive firestorm.

Fiery blasts of air shook buildings with stunning violence, knocking over chimneys and lifting off roofs. Trees, houses, barns, and even grass on lawns burst into flames, and all combustible items in the town, including thirteen hundred inhabitants, were consumed in the flames. Only ashes remained where rows of houses had stood. After destroying Peshtigo, the fire spread across northern Wisconsin and upper Michigan, eventually destroying 1,280,000 acres of timberland and killing an estimated fifteen hundred people.

The extremely violent fire that destroyed Peshtigo has been described as a "fire tornado." Many small fires that burned mostly surface vegetation without consuming the leaves of taller shrubs and trees had smoldered since September. It is possible that these fires, having established themselves over a large area without using up a significant proportion of the potential fuel, blazed up all at once with a sudden change in the weather. Radiated heat from two or more scattered but adjacent fires can suddenly ignite the combustible material in between. This can create a violent fire storm, appearing almost instantaneously, from what had seemed to be separate and far less alarming fires. Then, unaffected by local winds, the fire storm can act as an enormous chimney, producing a powerful column of rising hot air and drawing winds into the fire from all directions at great velocities. This may be what happened at Peshtigo.

Firestorms have other causes. Allied bombings during World War II also created some enormous fire storms. The attack on Hamburg, Germany, in 1943 started a firestorm with winds of 150 mph and temperatures over eighteen hundred degrees Fahrenheit.

Most who survived the Peshtigo fire were saved by jumping into the Peshtigo River. G. J. Tisdale was in the three-story Peshtigo Hotel when it caught fire. He ran out onto the porch, the wind caught him and hurled him through the air, and he found himself sprawled on the ground some distance from the building. As he ran toward the river, he was knocked down several more times by the wind and was stung by windblown sand that was so hot it burned his skin. Once he reached the river he could only keep his head above water for seconds at a time because the heat was so intense. He remembered seeing floating logs catch fire and burn down to the water line.

Some people in the river put coats or quilts over their heads to protect themselves from the heat. These cloaks dried quickly and had to be constantly dipped into the river. Others in the river constantly splashed water at each other. A priest in the river recalled the strange scene.

"The river was brighter than by day, and the spectacle presented by those heads rising above the level of the water —some covered, some uncovered—and the countless hands employed in beating the waves was singular and painful in the extreme. So free was I from the fear and anxiety that might naturally have been expected to reign in my mind at such a moment that I actually perceived only the ludicrous side of the scene at times and smiled within myself at it.

"When turning my gaze from the river, I saw nothing but flames. Houses, trees, and the air itself were on fire. Above my head—as far as the eye could reach into space—I saw nothing but immense volumes of flames covering the firmament, rolling one over the other with stormy violence as we see masses of clouds driven wildly hither and thither by the fierce power of the tempest."

Some families couldn't reach the river because of the flames and tried to escape the fire in plowed fields. Twenty-one women and children from three families huddled under a single large quilt to escape the burning embers swirling down out of the gale. The fathers, knowing it would cost their lives, stayed in the open, wetting down the cloth with water from buckets that they had carried with them. The men's clothes were burned off their bodies. In the morning the fathers were all dead, but the twenty-one women and children under the scorched quilt all survived.

The Peshtigo fire, although the worst forest fire in the history of the United States, is little known today. This is partly because the Peshtigo blaze was eclipsed by a far more famous fire—the Great Chicago Fire, which took place on the same day and at almost the same hour.

A deadly train ride through a forest fire

In September 1894, twenty-three years after the Peshtigo fire, a rampaging forest fire burned across northern Minnesota, killing 418 people and destroying twelve towns. Just before the flames reached Hinckley, Minnesota, most of its inhabitants escaped aboard two freight trains. A third train, the daily passenger train from Duluth, arrived to find the outskirts of the town already blazing. Engineer Jim Root found a crowd of two hundred terrified people waiting at the depot for the train to take them to safety. They climbed aboard and Root headed down the track toward St. Paul, Minnesota. Soon the train reached an impassible wall of fire, and with the engine cab and baggage car starting to burn, the engineer jammed on the brakes, threw the locomotive into reverse, and roared backward through the town in a desperate attempt to outrun the fire. The flames had reached the track, and soon even the ties burst into flame. Root's fireman first dived into the train's water tank to escape flames shooting into the cab. Then, seeing that the engineer's denim's were beginning to burn, he came out again and began throwing buckets of water on Root.

Inside the train a porter named John W. Blair made the passengers lie down on the car floors when the fierce heat shattered the windows and set the woodwork afire. As he walked up and down the train, he poured water on the heads and clothing of women and children.

After the train had traveled six miles through the conflagration, it reached Skunk Pond, a muddy pool that promised salvation. Root fell unconscious from his burns after he had braked the train, but the grateful passengers carried him to safety in the water. They huddled in the pond for twelve hours as the fire raged around them.

The thankful survivors honored the porter, John W. Blair, at a party in St. Paul, and the railroad company gave him a gold watch for "gallant and faithful discharge of duty." Root, the engineer, was bedridden for months by his burns.

CHAPTER 15

Struck By Lightning

*N*icky Schneider, an eleven-year-old member of an Arlington, Texas, boy's soccer team, was dashing downfield after the ball just as rain began to splatter down from a darkening thunderstorm in April 1984. Suddenly, horrified spectators saw the boy's body silhouetted in the brilliant blue-white flash of a bolt of lightning. As Nicky's paralyzed body fell to the ground, others, standing nearby, were knocked backward onto the mud and grass by a blast of air rushing away from the murderous bolt.

Two women, one an X-ray technologist and the other just two months short of graduating from medical school, ran to the fallen boy and saw wisps of smoke coming out of his mouth and ears. An ugly welt on his scalp showed where the bolt had entered his body. Nicky had burn marks down his left side and the tops of his shoes had been blown off. Most horrifying of all, he had no pulse. One woman began to give Nicky mouth-to-mouth resuscitation while the other pumped at his chest. Ten minutes later, when firemen and paramedics arrived with respiration equipment, the two women, feeling no pulse, thought that they had lost their fight to save the boy's life.

As the current jolted down through Nicky's body it

passed through the respiratory center, located in the lower part of the brain, and stopped his breathing. Then the sizzling current, continuing its deadly course toward Nicky's feet, passed through his heart and stopped its beating, either by causing ventricular fibrillation or cardiac arrest. When the lightning current flowed over the surface of Nicky's feet on its way into the ground, his skin moisture and sweat were turned into steam, and the resulting pressure of expansion in his tight-fitting shoes blew them apart. Some other accounts of lightning-strike victims, including a few who survived, have told of their clothes or shoes being exploded off their bodies. For example, two farm girls were standing by a reaping machine when lightning struck. The bolt stripped them to the skin and ripped their boots off, but they were unhurt.

After Nicky's body had been lifted into an ambulance, the paramedics detected a faint, slow pulse that kept getting stronger as time passed. In the hospital, the comatose boy was kept breathing with the aid of a ventilator. His doctors soon decided that the greatest cause of concern was damage in Nicky's brain. A blood clot, surrounded by swollen tissue, had formed deep in the brain in an area that controls motor function. However, as the days passed, the clot slowly dissolved and the swelling lessened.

Twelve days after being struck, Nicky regained consciousness. He couldn't speak intelligibly or control his movements. But, after a slow recuperation lasting many months, Nicky made a complete recovery.

How had Nicky survived a direct lightning strike that could have produced a current as great as thirty million volts (compared to household current of 110 to 220 volts), and heat as high as thirty thousand to fifty thousand degrees Fahrenheit? Such strikes are almost always fatal. One clue could be seen in the second-degree burns that covered one-eighth of his body. Nicky was soaked by rain when struck, and the thin film of water on the surface of his body may have conducted most of the current to the ground.

A few other victims of direct lightning strikes have survived when the tremendous surge of current moving down through their body met a larger electrical resistance than that traveling through the surrounding air. A large part of the current flashed from the body and arced through the air down to the ground. This can reduce the remaining flow of current through the body to a survivable level. However, the clothes may burst into flame at the site of the flash over to the ground. Lightning has, on occasion, struck umbrellas, golf clubs, or pitch forks held above victim's heads. In these cases the current pathway will miss the brain, instead passing from the hand holding the conductor, through the trunk, and generally via the feet to the earth.

Surviving all types of lightning strikes

Although nearly all victims of *direct* lightning strikes are killed, about two-thirds of all victims of lightning accidents survive. This happens because current from a lightning bolt often reaches its victim by other means than a direct strike. If a person is in contact with the conducting object when it is struck—a bolt of lightning sending its electrical charge through the telephone wire or plumbing for example—the result may or may not be fatal. A Charlotte, North Carolina, woman was drawing a glass of water from the tap for one of her children when a bolt of lightning sent a charge of electricity along the water pipe. She was knocked to the floor, and when asked if she was hurt, she replied, "No, but I am turning blind." She died a few minutes later, probably from ventricular fibrillation or cardiac arrest.

If a victim is standing close to, but not touching, an object struck by lightning, a part of the current may cross the air gap and discharge to earth through him. This may also be fatal. Two soldiers entered a tent shortly before it was struck by lightning during World War II. The current flashed off the tent pole, killing one of the men immediately. He had superficial burns on the left shoulder, hip, and thigh, indicating that the current had entered at the shoulder and passed down his body through the heart on its way to the ground. The other man, who survived, had a burn only on his left thigh, showing that the current had lept from the pole to his thigh and passed down through his body below the heart, thus allowing him to escape death.

Many escapes from electrocution have resulted from current flowing through the body along a path that *misses* such vital organs as the heart. In a non-lightning electrical accident in the mid-1950s, while working in his shirt sleeves, an operator in a small broadcasting studio noticed that a high voltage tube was tilted slightly to one side. When he tried to straighten it, the glass broke and his hand touched the high-voltage assembly in the center of the tube. With one hand on the high-voltage current and the other grounded on the transmitter, the paralyzing current prevented him from removing his hands. The current pathway was across his chest and heart, and he was only instants away from electrocution.

Thinking fast, he twisted his arms so that his bare elbows touched. This created a short circuit so that the current no longer flowed across his chest but instead jumped from hand to hand through his elbows. He pulled himself away and collapsed from shock. But he was able to return to work in a week.

Another way that a lightning bolt can shock is by voltage generated in the ground near the strike. This can happen in some cases where the lightning-struck object is too far away to generate a side flash through the air to the victim. The amount of current flowing through the victim depends on the difference in lightning-caused electrification of the ground under the foot nearest to the strike, compared to the smaller electrification of the ground under the foot farther from the strike. Because the feet of a human are relatively close together, the difference in the electrification of ground under the two feet is relatively small and the current tends to be fairly weak. The current will flow up the leg nearest to the strike, through the lower part of the trunk, and down the other leg on its path back into the ground. Little if any current will flow through the heart or brain, and death from this type of lightning effect is very rare. However, cattle or horses, with much greater distance between their legs, will have stronger currents flowing through their bodies and often are killed by such a nearby strike.

Horseracing fans at Britain's Ascot race course were shocked one day when lightning struck and electrified the surface on which they were standing. Many were thrown to the ground and found themselves unable to rise when they tried to move their legs. Out of fifty-one people taken to a hospital, twenty, complaining of pains in their legs, had to be detained.

In another case, a French church was struck during a service. All those standing on damp flagstones in the nave of the church fell and were unable to get up for several minutes until the temporary paralysis in their legs left them. Others, insulated from the current by standing in the oak choir section at the side, were untouched by the electricity.

Dr. H. A. Spencer recorded an unusual case of ground-current effects in his book *Lightning, Lightning Stroke and its Treatment* (Balliere, Tyndall, & Cox, 1932).

"An elderly gentleman and his son were walking arm-in-arm one night, outside their hotel, on the outskirts of a village in the Transvaal (in northeastern South Africa), when a flash of lightning struck the ground two hundred yards away from them, just as they were walking over an outcrop of ironstone. They received a shock that threw them to the ground locked in one another's embrace, and they rolled about on the ground for some minutes, unable to disentangle themselves or to call out. Finally, some people outside the hotel, thinking they were fighting, separated them and assisted them to their feet, still unable to explain what had occurred. Arriving on the scene soon afterward, I found that they had regained their power of speech and were able to discuss the occurrence. They explained that their legs had suddenly ceased to support them and they found themselves rolling upon the ground with flexed limbs. . . . Neither of them showed any burns or *other* evidence of having been struck by lightning, but their muscles were cramped and sore. . . . Next morning, on visiting the spot where the lightning had struck the ground, I found an outcrop of ironstone similar to that outside the hotel; as I was able to trace it across the intervening ground without difficulty, it must have been continuous."

The two men, walking arm-in-arm and straddling a considerable length of the conducting ironstone vein, had picked up a strong current between the right foot of one man and the left foot of the other, similar to the strong current that would have occured between the widely spread legs of cattle or horses. Because of the effect of foot spread on current strength, people who are caught in open spaces during lightning storms are advised to crouch down with their feet close together.

Getting zapped on the golf course

One of the most well-known survivors of a lightning bolt is Lee Trevino, the professional golfer and television golf announcer. During the Western Open near Chicago in June 1975, Trevino and two other touring professional golfers were zapped painfully but non-fatally. After burns on his shoulder had healed, Trevino returned to tournament golf, but with a self-professed change in attitude. "If I shoot a 77, I don't give a damn anymore. At least it doesn't upset me as much as it used to. Something like that is an experience you never forget. Emotionally, it shook me up."

Golfers are a favorite victim of lightning bolts, and some have been shocked more than once. Jim Davey, the pro at the Bobby Jones municipal course in Atlanta, survived two strikes. The second time he saw sparks fly out of his wedge and he suffered some painful after effects. "It burned the bottoms of my feet and my insides shook for three days." Another time, playing on the nearby Piedmont Park course, he wasn't struck but still had a frighteningly close brush with death. "While I was waiting for the green up ahead to clear, the fellow playing behind me hit and his ball rolled between my legs," Davey recollected. "I went ahead, but that man was struck by the lightning and killed right where I'd been standing just seconds before."

Another Atlanta golfer, Mac Sams, Jr., was struck twice in 1975. The first bolt merely shattered his umbrella as he was running toward the clubhouse. But a second strike, later in the year, killed two of his playing partners, knocked him cold under "some damned persimmon trees," and left him temporarily unable to recall his own name. "I never knew what hit us," said Sams. "I was standing there one minute commenting about how wet my pants were and the next thing I knew, I was flat on the ground and couldn't even move."

Major league pitcher struck on mound

The only major league baseball pitcher ever to be knocked down by lightning during a game was Ray "Slim" Caldwell of the Cleveland Indians in 1919. Slim, a fine pitcher but much too fond of whiskey, had already been released by two teams because of his drinking problems. Tris Speaker, the Cleveland manager and one of the finest center fielders of all time, didn't want the trouble of trying to stop Caldwell's drinking so he used another approach. He decided not to attempt to stop his drinking but to limit his sprees to non-critical times. He offered Slim Caldwell a very generous contract and when Slim eagerly agreed to sign it, Speaker cautioned, "I told you to read this contract very carefully. You've looked only at the money. Now read every word of it."

Slim began to read the contract.

"After each game he pitches, Ray Caldwell must get drunk. He is not to report to the clubhouse the next day. The second day he is to report to Manager Speaker and run around the ball park as many times as Manager Speaker stipulates. The third day he is to pitch batting practice, and the fourth day he is to pitch in a championship [quality] game."

Slim looked up in amazement. "You left out one word, Tris," he said. "Where it says I've got to get drunk after each game, the word 'not' has been left out. It should read that I'm 'not to get drunk.'"

Speaker smiled, "No, it says you *are* to get drunk."

Slim enthusiastically signed the contract. Soon afterward he was pitching in Philadelphia with two out in the ninth inning and one strike called on the last batter. A lightning bolt suddenly crashed to earth near the pitcher's mound, flattening Slim and knocking him unconscious for five minutes. He was resuscitated by first aid, stood up, and told Manager Speaker that he was all right, though a bit dizzy. The newly revived Slim then whipped two more strikes by the batter to end the game!

Human lightning rod

People who have survived one or even two lightning bolts are completely overshadowed by former Virginia Park Ranger Roy Sullivan. Sullivan, the world record holder for lightning strikes (according to Guinness), was struck seven times. He was first zapped in 1942, losing his big toe nail. In 1969 his eyebrows were scorched, in 1970 his shoulder was seared, and in 1972 his hair was set on fire—all by lightning strikes. In 1973 as he was stepping out of a truck, he received his most severe strike. "It set my hat and hair on fire," he recalled. "Then it went down my left arm and leg, knocked off my shoe, and crossed over to my right leg. It also set my underwear on fire." He poured a bucket of water over his head to cool off. In 1976 he was struck a sixth time and his ankle was injured. In 1977, while fishing, he attracted another bolt and went to the hospital with chest and stomach burns. Sullivan donated his lightning-burnt Ranger hats to the Guinness World Records exhibits in New York City and Myrtle Beach. This apparently indestructible man was felled by his own hand when he shot himself in September, 1983, because of a reported rejection in love.

Pranks played by lightning

While it could hardly be pleasant to be electrified by lightning, Gretel Ehrlich, in her book *The Solace of Open Spaces*, recalled the experience of being shocked by a bolt in this way: "It felt as though sequins had been poured down my legs." Sometimes lightning also plays mischievous pranks on people without injuring them. Some of these are accomplished by the violent wave of compressed air that is driven outward from a lightning flash. This can hurl people a dozen feet or more. In one case lightning struck a room where a girl was sitting at a sewing machine with a scissors in her hand. There was a brilliant flash, the scissors were spirited away, and the girl found herself sitting *on* the sewing machine. In another case a farm laborer was carrying a pitchfork when the blast from a nearby lightning strike flung it fifty yards away and twisted the tines into corkscrews. A man's drink from a mug was interrupted when a blast of air from a lightning bolt hurled the mug into a nearby courtyard. The startled man was uninjured. Two women, quietly knitting, had their needles snatched out of their hands in another lightning strike incident.

The intense heat from a lightning bolt has also played some good tricks on victims who were left uninjured but very surprised. The *United States Safety Council's Report* for 1943 tells of a soldier who was welded into his sleeping bag when lightning struck the zipper. Lightning can also do strange things to inanimate objects. Lightning once struck a chain maker's shop, soldering all the links in a yard-long chain and turning another chain into a bar of iron. On another occasion lightning set fire to a building and then struck and set off a nearby fire alarm, thus calling out the fire brigade to extinguish the blaze.

CHAPTER 16

Riding in Tornadoes

W*ho was* the first human ever to take off from the ground, soar up through the sky, and then land safely? We will never know because that pioneer flier undoubtedly made the flight far back in prehistory in the most dangerous and terrifying manner of flying—inside a tornado funnel. There are some remarkable accounts of more recent cases where people have gone aloft in tornadoes and survived. Meteorologists from the United States Weather Bureau (now the National Weather Service) carefully investigated many of these unusual accounts—checking out not only the reports themselves, but also the reliability of the observers—and concluded that some most extraordinary stories are true.

One such incident (considered well-authenticated by investigating Weather Bureau officials) occurred in April 1947, when two Texans, Al and Bill (last names not given in the report) were visiting in Al's home near Higgins, Texas. Al's wife and two children were sitting close to the two men. Suddenly Al heard a tremendous roar approaching the house and stepped to the door and opened it to see what was coming. He was pulled out of the doorway by a tornado and carried away over the treetops. Bill rushed to the door to look for Al and soon found himself also sailing up through the air, but in a slightly different direction than his friend was heading.

Both men landed about two hundred feet from the house with only minor injuries. Al started back toward his house and found Bill uncomfortably wrapped up in wire. He unwound Bill and then they began to crawl toward the house because the wind was so strong that the men couldn't walk against it. They reached the spot where Al's home had been, but all of the house had disappeared except for the floor. The two Texans found Al's wife and two children huddled on a divan, uninjured. The only other piece of furniture left on the floor was a lamp.

A similar incident took place near Ponca City, Oklahoma, in April 1925. A tornado picked up a house in which a farmer and his wife were eating dinner and carried it aloft. The house literally exploded in the air, but the floor platform on which they were still seated, clutching the table between them, settled horizontally to earth and the couple stepped off, uninjured.

How are such flights possible? Upcurrents in the tornado may be 150 mph or more in velocity, capable of lifting enormous weights. A tornado caught up with a passenger train in May 1931, about five miles east of Moorhead, Minnesota, while the train was speeding down the track at almost sixty miles an hour. Five of the coaches, each weighing about seventy tons, were lifted from the track. One was carried eighty feet and dumped into a ditch. One man was killed and 57 of the 117 passengers on the train were injured.

The uprushing currents near the center of a tornado have enormous lifting power, but there is much less upward movement of wind near the outer part of the circulation. A person, animal, or object may thus be lifted rapidly off the ground in the strongest updraft and then be tossed into a portion of the twister where upcurrents only just fail to maintain the weight aloft, allowing a gentle descent to the ground.

In September 1981, a four-month-old baby, asleep in a

baby carriage outside his parents' home in Ancona, Italy, was lifted fifty feet in the air by a tornado and then lowered gently onto a road three-hundred feet away. The baby was still asleep.

A tornado totally demolished a small schoolhouse containing sixteen pupils in 1925. The children were carried 150 yards but none of them were killed.

In 1835 a twelve-year-old boy in New Brunswick, New Jersey, was reportedly carried from his father's home at the head of New Street down to the wharf, a distance of half a mile. He passed through a tree, the branches of which he tried to grasp, and landed with no injuries other than a strained wrist suffered when he grabbed at the tree.

A small tornado near Topeka, Kansas, lifted up a farm hand and set him down a hundred feet away, unharmed except for a coating of mud. His employer remarked that this was the fastest move he had ever seen the man make.

A man lifted in a tornado funnel at Wichita Falls, Texas, glimpsed objects in the funnel, just as the fictional character Dorothy in *The Wizard of Oz* did. A truck trailer rotated near him, and flying ahead of him was a mattress. "If I could reach that," he thought in his confused state of mind, "I'd just go to sleep." He then lost consciousness and woke up on the ground rolled up in barbed wire, punctured, but still very lucky to have escaped death.

Tornado rides usually do not end so fortunately. When a tornado struck Worcester, Massachusetts, in 1953, a woman went outside the house to call the dog. Her husband reported that, "She opened the door and that is the last we saw of her. She just went up into the air and out of sight." In 1925 a rural school teacher was carried away to her death by a tornado while her pupils, clinging to their desks, were not seriously injured.

Tricks played by tornadoes

Tornadoes have done some extraordinary jobs of moving inanimate objects without breaking them. A Kansas tornado carried a dresser more than one hundred yards and set it down by a wire fence without breaking the glass mirror.

A tornado at Fergus Falls, Minnesota, in June 1915, performed some remarkable pranks. The twister split a large tree and lifted an automobile into the crack. The split then closed, holding the car as tightly as though it were in a vise. Also in the same storm a cut-glass vase was carried from its resting place on a buffet, over a stack of dishes, and around a corner into another room without being broken.

On another occasion a house was ripped apart by a tornado that carried off the kitchen cupboard, filled with dishes, and set it down so gently that not a dish was broken. A tornado once carried a jar of pickles twenty-five miles and lowered it, unbroken, into a ditch. And a pair of pants with the pockets containing a Kansas farmer's fourteen hundred dollar down payment on the sale of his farm was found—along with a dead hog, a pump, and a washing machine—in a nearby cave.

After a tornado at Tupelo, Mississippi, in April 1936, a minister near Cherokee, Alabama, sixty miles away, found a photograph with a woman's name on it that had evidently been blown clear from Tupelo. He mailed it back to the woman who was then hospitalized with injuries caused by the tornado. She replied that the photo had been in a trunk in the hallway of her home. The tornado had blown open the trunk and picked up the photograph. The house had been demolished, the woman's five-year-old daughter killed, and her husband severely injured.

A tornado coming from the northwest near Cottonwood Falls, Kansas, passed over a north-south barbed-wire fence nearly a mile long. All the fence posts were yanked out of the ground and the fence, posts and all, was rolled up as neatly as if the work had been done painstakingly by hand.

A prime source of tornado lifting power and destructiveness is the lowered air pressure in the funnel compared to the air pressure outside the tornado. This is caused by the centrifugal force of the whirl.

The suction effect of tornadoes is responsible for some strange incidents. Four miners were returning home from their jobs in March 1925, when their car suddenly began to bounce along the road in Princeton, Indiana. The doors popped open and all four men were pulled from the car as if by a huge, invisible hand. The tornado dropped them, unhurt, alongside the road, but tore their car into small pieces that were scattered along several miles of highway.

A tornado near Harveyville, Kansas, passed close to a farm house and drew the bedding and mattress from under a sleeping boy without injuring him, according to a story told to a Weather Bureau official by the boy's father shortly after the storm. The oil from a kerosene lamp on a nearby dresser was sucked out and sprayed over the room without breaking either the lamp or its chimney. The Weather Bureau official reported that the room still reeked of kerosene at the time of his visit. The partial vacuum causes corks to fly out of bottles, soot to be sucked out of chimneys, bark to be plucked off trees, harnesses to be stripped off horses, and clothes off human beings, often leaving people totally naked.

The suction has also demonstrated its power in wells and rivers. A farmer's wife left two buckets of milk hanging in a well to cool—a common practice in earlier times. A tornado lifted them both up out of the well and departed with them. Tornadoes have sucked ropes, buckets, and water out of open wells. A tornado sucked up a river and left the riverbed momentarily dry when it passed over the West Fork River in West Virginia, in June 1944.

Another reason why tornadoes can create many notable narrow escapes is that the distance between the violent winds in the funnel and calmer ones at the storm perimeter may be small, especially if the funnel is long with a narrow tip. The horizontal whirling winds at the base of the funnel may exceed 250 mph. Sand and gravel are blown with such force that they bore into human bodies like bullets. Wheat straws are commonly shot deep into the bark of trees. In one well-documented case, a two-by-four pine plank was blown clear through a five-eighths inch thick solid iron girder supporting the Eads Bridge in St. Louis.

There are reports of a flower forced into the fiber of a wooden plank, undamaged candles embedded deep in the plaster walls of rooms, and even an egg with a bean blown into the yoke through a neat hole in an otherwise uncracked shell. Trees, sides of buildings, and even people are often covered so tightly by violently-flung mud that it is very difficult to remove.

When the lethal whirling winds are combined with the destructive effects of suction and updrafts, a tornado may totally destroy a house while another house next door, just out of range of the destructive funnel, remains undamaged.

A group of California tourists were driving toward Topeka, Kansas, in June 1917, when they saw a tornado roaring toward them. Although they could have driven out of the funnel's path, they left the car and ran to get shelter in a nearby schoolhouse. The school was locked, so they all went into a small, flimsy coal shed at the rear of the school building. The tornado totally destroyed the schoolhouse and blew away a building located within two feet of the coal shed. The shed was practically undamaged and the tourists escaped without a scratch. Their car was rolled several hundred feet down the highway and turned into junk.

In March 1948, in Gillespie, Illinois, a woman heard a tornado coming and ran to get her child out of bed. The two sought shelter in a clothes closet under a back stairway. After the tornado passed, the woman opened the closet door and saw that the closet and stairway were all that remained of the house. Neither she nor her child had been injured.

A tornado at Pryor, Oklahoma, blew away every splinter of a house except for the front porch and a wooden bench in April 1942. The left rear wheel of an automobile parked near the porch was blown away, but a kerosene lamp was still intact, lighted, and burning under a nearby tree.

A man was driving a horse-drawn, heavily loaded wagon in St. Louis in May 1896, when a tornado carried away the horses leaving behind the wagon and the uninjured man. There is also a record of a cow being carried away while being milked. The baffled person doing the milking was left sitting beside where the cow had just been.

On one extraordinary occasion a whole group of cattle were spotted drifting off together through the air "looking like gigantic birds in the sky." A meteorologist later described the incident as "the herd shot around the world." And a Louisiana rooster was carried several miles in a tornado and set down in a flock of hens, "still full of strut and fight."

The stories reported about tornadoes and freak incidents certainly sound like "tall tales," and many would seem completely unbelievable if it had not been for the investigations of U.S. government meteorologists. Two stories which are certainly not true are one of an iron kettle that was turned inside out without cracking and another that told of a rooster blown into a jug with only his head sticking out.

Looking inside a tornado funnel

A tornado is one of the most awesome sights that a person can ever see. Some observers have had extraordinary close-up views of funnels while remaining safely on the ground. A Kansas farmer, Will Keller, described his view of the inside of a tornado to the official in charge of the Weather Bureau Office at Dodge City, Kansas.

"On the afternoon of June 22, 1928, between three and four o'clock, I noticed an umbrella-shaped cloud in the west and southwest, and from its appearance suspected that there was a tornado in it. The air had that peculiar oppressiveness that nearly always precedes the coming of a tornado.

"I saw at once my suspicions were correct. Hanging from the greenish black base of the cloud were three tornadoes. One was perilously near and apparently headed directly for my place. I lost no time in hurrying with my family to our cyclone cellar.

"The family had entered the cellar and I was in the doorway just about to enter when I decided I would take a last look at the approaching cloud. I have seen a number of these and did not lose my head, though the approaching tornado was an impressive sight.

"The surrounding country is level and there was nothing to obscure the sight. Two of the tornadoes were some distance away and looked like great ropes hanging from the parent cloud, but the one nearest was shaped more like a funnel, with ragged clouds surrounding it. It appeared larger than the others and occupied the central position, with great cumulus clouds over it.

"Steadily the cloud came on, the end gradually rising above the ground. I probably stood there only a few seconds but was so impressed with the sight it seemed like a long time. At last the great shaggy end of the funnel hung directly overhead. Everything was still as death. There was a strong gassy odor, and it seemed as though I could not breathe. There was a screaming, hissing sound coming directly from the end of the funnel. I looked up, and to my astonishment I saw right into the heart of the tornado. There was a circular opening in the center of the funnel, about fifty to one hundred feet in diameter and extending straight upward for a distance of at least half a mile, as best I could judge under the circumstances. The walls of this opening were rotating clouds and the hole was brilliantly lighted with constant flashes of lightning, which zigzagged from side to side. Had it not been for the lightning, I could not have seen the opening, or any distance into it.

"Around the rim of the vortex small tornadoes were constantly forming and breaking away. These looked like tails as they writhed their way around the funnel. It was these that made the hissing sound. I noticed the rotation of the great whirl was anticlockwise, but some of the small twisters rotated clockwise. The opening was entirely hollow, except for something I could not exactly make out but suppose it was a detached wind cloud. This thing kept moving up and down. The tornado was not traveling at great speed. I had plenty of time to get a good view of the whole thing, inside and out. Its course was not in a straight line, but it zigzagged across the country, in a general northeasterly direction.

"After it passed my place it again dipped and struck and demolished the house and barn of a farmer by the name of Evans. The Evans family, like ourselves, had been looking over their hailed out wheat and saw the tornado coming. Not having time to reach their cellar they took refuge under a small bluff that faced to the leeward of the approaching tornado. They lay down flat on the ground and caught hold of some plum bushes, which fortunately grew within their reach. Mr. Evans said that he could see the wreckage of his house, among it being the cook stove, going round and round over his head."

In more recent times meteorologists have not had to rely solely on interviews with witnesses such as Will Keller. Since 1974, meteorologists from institutions such as the National Severe Storm Laboratory in Norman, Oklahoma, have been chasing tornadoes in their vehicles, making films at close range, and placing weather instruments in what they guess will be the storm's path. They hope to learn how to better predict such storms and save lives. William Hauptman, a writer traveling along with a team of tornado chasers, got a close-up look at a tornado.

"Jets of dust leap up and scissor around the mouth of the funnel, which seems to be made of dense black fluid instead of air. It looks larger than any moving thing should be.

"The tornado is simply the most spectacular thing I have ever seen. I feel euphoria. I am watching forces that operate on a scale beyond my imagination. When the funnel comes so close that it fills the viewfinder of my camera, I let the camera drop and stare."

Although some may be fascinated or even euphoric while viewing a tornado at close range, many are traumatized by a tornado disaster. William Bixby in his book *Havoc: The Story of Natural Disasters*, described common reactions of survivors after their town, Irving, Kansas, was devastated by a tornado.

"So shocked were the people who lived through the storm that the memory of it remained like that of a gigantic nightmare for months and years afterward. Many could not look on the normal darkness of an approaching evening without peering into the dusk apprehensively, fearful that another such storm would come upon them with impenetrable might. During the daytime, sudden gusts of wind or the shadow of a dark cloud could turn the survivors into statues of fear, so terrifying had been the experience."

CHAPTER 17

Dodging Mayhem

O*n November 15, 1884*, John Lee, a twenty-year-old English footman, was standing on a gallows with his arms pinioned behind his back, a white bag over his head, and a noose around his neck. Lee was about to be hanged for the murder of his wealthy employer, Miss Emma Ann Keyse. The executioner was James Berry, a former policeman whose varied career also included the occupations of shopkeeper, showman, lecturer, auctioneer, lay preacher, and farmer.

"Have you anything to say?" Berry asked in a whisper as he tightened the knot.

"No," replied Lee, "drop away!"

The hangman pulled the bolt that would release the trap door and send John Lee dropping to his death. The trap door dropped only about two inches and Lee stood on tiptoe with the noose tight around his neck. Lee didn't utter a sound.

After about five minutes the noose was removed, and Lee was led away to an adjacent storeroom where the cap over his head was removed. He heard men opening and shutting the trapdoor. A prison officer was testing the gallows by hanging from the rope with his hands. When the bolt was withdrawn, the trap door worked perfectly.

Lee was led back to the scaffold to finish the grisly business. Executioner Berry, however, was in a state of nervous collapse. "My poor fellow," he exclaimed to Lee, "I don't know what I am doing."

Once more they bound and blindfolded Lee and put the noose around his neck and once more Berry pulled the bolt. But again the trap door only dropped two inches. This time Lee was pushed back a couple of paces and stood pinioned and blindfolded while the prison officials desperately tested the mechanism.

At last all was ready and Lee was placed for the third time on the drop. The bolt was drawn and Lee for the third time felt the nightmarish fall begin and then quickly end as the trap door stopped after dropping only inches, leaving Lee dangling on the tips of his toes, unable to see, half-suffocated and half-hung.

Lee was untied and his hood removed. The prison doctor offered him a glass of brandy, but Lee declined it. "My poor fellow," Berry cried out, "how you have had to suffer."

John Lee was taken back to his cell while unnerved government officials wondered what to do. Finally, Lee's sentence was commuted to life in prison, and after serving over twenty-two years he was given his freedom in 1907. After an unsuccessful marriage he became a London junk dealer.

What had happened? The official explanation was that recent rains had caused the planks of the trap to swell so that it jammed every time a weight was put on it. Frank Ross, an ex-convict, gave another explanation. He claimed that the gallows had been built by a master joiner who was serving a life sentence for murder after having been reprieved from hanging. Ross stated that the joiner had constructed the gallows so that the trap door wouldn't open during an actual hanging because the chaplain would be standing on a board that jammed the trap.

The experience had a bad effect on James Berry, the executioner. Berry began to think that the hand of Providence had prevented him from hanging an innocent man (many other superstitious people also believed this). Years after he publicly announced that he felt certain he had hanged several innocent people. After he retired from hanging people Berry became a lay preacher and expressed the hope that he would live to see the day when hanging would be abolished from England. Berry died in 1913.

During the Second World War, Ronald Seth had an experience similar to John Lee's when the Germans tried to hang him as a spy in Estonia. He recollected the experience:

"The trap on which I was standing suddenly gave beneath my feet, fell a few inches, and then stuck. I heard shouts and saw blurred figures running hither and thither. Then I fell forward. The rope tightened behind my ears, and my eyes were filled with bright lights and then darkness. It was early afternoon when I came to and found myself back in cell thirteen."

The explanation for this unexpected reprieve was that the guards had been drunk with vodka to warm themselves in the cold climate, and some anti-Nazis took advantage of the guards' alcoholized state to "fix" the gallows so that the trap would stick. Seth survived and in 1952 wrote a book about the experience entitled *A Spy Has No Friend*.

Condemned prisoners have escaped hanging by other means. As the trap door dropped beneath Will Purvis, a nineteen-year-old Mississippi farmer and convicted murderer, in 1894, the rope around his neck unwound and he dropped safely to the ground. Officials were about to hang Purvis a second time when a preacher asked for a show of hands of "all who are opposed to hanging Will Purvis a second time." Hundreds of hands rose and the crowd moved forward menacingly toward the officials. Purvis was returned to his cell.

After a time, the Mississippi Supreme Court ruled that Purvis had to be executed, but before the hanging could take place a group of Purvis's friends helped him to escape. Purvis emerged from hiding in 1896 after A. J. McLaurin was elected governor. McLaurin had promised to commute

Purvis's sentence to life imprisonment. Purvis was pardoned in 1898 after the murder victim's brother, who had previously identified Purvis as the murderer, admitted that he was not sure that Purvis had been the killer.

In 1917, twenty-four years after the murder, a dying man named Joe Beard confessed to the crime at a religious revival meeting. Beard stated that he and another man were the killers. Beard provided enough evidence to show that he had information only the real murderer or murderers would have known. In 1920 the Mississippi legislature awarded Will Purvis five-thousand dollars compensation "for a great wrong done you" and removed "all stain and dishonor from your name."

In the earlier years of hangings, condemned prisoners were not killed by falling from a trap door to break the victim's neck, but rather had the support pulled from under them and were left to dangle in the air. Sometimes victims were cut down and then found to be still alive. William Duell was hanged at Tyburn near London in 1740 for murder. He was cut down, but a few hours later, it was noticed that he was breathing. He was not hanged a second time but instead was sent off to the colonies.

Another survivor of hanging was "Half-Hangit" Maggie Dickson. After being hanged at the public market in Edinburgh, Scotland, in 1728, she was cut down, placed in a coffin, and driven in a cart to her home at Musselburgh, about nine miles from where she had been hanged. During the bumpy ride she came back to life. After surviving the hanging she was pardoned and lived to be a very old woman, with many children. When strangers visited Musselburgh, they were told the story of "Half-Hangit" Maggie Dickson, and she was pointed out to them if in view.

There have also been narrow escapes from other types of executions. Jim Williams was waiting for his execution in a Florida electric chair when an argument started between Warden James S. Blitch and Sheriff R. J. Hancock in 1926. Each insisted that it was the other's duty to throw the switch. The argument went on for twenty minutes until Williams finally collapsed. He was carried back to his cell and the dispute continued in the courts. Eventually a court ruled that the sheriff had to pull the switch, but by then the Board of Pardons decided that Williams's sentence should be commuted to life imprisonment.

F. Yeats-Brown gave an account of a narrow escape from the guillotine during the French Revolution in his book *Escape*. An aristocrat was walking behind an over-crowded tumbrel to the place of execution when he found himself separated by chance from the other victims. He was handcuffed but became lost in the crowd. For some time he could not believe his luck. He strolled into a cafe where he told a stranger that friends had bound his hands together and taken away his money as a joke. He added that if the stranger would help free his hands and then take a note to a nearby friend of his, the stranger would be well rewarded. The stranger agreed and the aristocrat was soon safely in hiding.

Close calls with bullets

While a few people have escaped death while in the process of being executed, countless others have had re-prieves from the lethal effects of projectiles such as bullets, artillery shells, and bombs. Some of the most unusual of the vast number of bullet wounds survived in wartime in-volved bullets that lodged in the victim's hearts before the days of open heart surgery. When the bullet did not create an open wound or block the heart's flow, patients often made a good immediate recovery, often without significant symptoms, even though the bullet was lodged in the heart. This generally happened when a spent bullet entered the heart with low velocity. In some cases bullets remained in victim's hearts for many years without any problems. Dr. G. Grey Turner, the former director of the Department of Surgery, British Postgraduate Medical School, wrote in 1940 about one of his cases, a man who had been shot in the heart in 1916 while serving in World War I.

"The patient was an officer, thirty-two years of age,

who was wounded by a machine-gun bullet fired at a range of about five-hundred yards. There was a snowstorm at the time and the officer had his left hand up to keep the snow from his eyes, and as there was a through-and-through wound just above the elbow, it is highly probable that the bullet that lodged in the heart first passed through the arm. In addition it traversed a notebook and a bundle of letters that he was carrying in his tunic pocket. The officer did not appear to have been very severely knocked out after the wound, and when I saw him at the base eighteen days later he was not in any way upset and was rather ashamed that he perforce arrived on a stretcher. The wound of entrance was through the front of the cardiac area and there was no exit. The radiograph showed the bullet in the region of the left ventricle. It was pulsating synchronously with the heartbeat, and in addition there was a whirling movement as if its apex was spinning about in the vortex of the blood stream. After due consideration I made an attempt to move the bullet, but without success. Now [1940], twenty-four years after the injury, the patient remains perfectly well and is able to live a normal, reasonably active life."

How did the man survive the heart wound? The lodged bullet could have acted as a plug to prevent hemmorhaging or the firm contraction of the powerful muscular walls of the ventricles could have stopped bleeding until healing took place. Some other survivors with bullets lodged in their heart had more serious after-effects. The bullets sometimes became dislodged and left the cardiac cavity. They could form emboli in main vessels. Scars associated with bullets sometimes gave way and caused the sudden death of the victims. Also the lodged bullets sometimes caused great cardiac irregularity and difficulties in breathing. Dr. Turner, writing in the early 1940s, recommended exploratory surgery to see if bullets lodged in the heart could be removed. Now such removal can almost always be readily done.

In 1852 Sir John Packington fought a pistol duel with John Parker. Neither man was injured, but the bullet from Parker's gun neatly clipped off part of Sir John's whiskers.

In 1900 Mock Duck, the greatest tong warrior ever to appear in any American Chinatown, was the victim of an assassination attempt. One bullet grazed the Chinese gangster's coat and another hit him square in the midsection. Mock Duck, who survived many assassination attempts, escaped injury when the bullet struck his massive belt buckle. In 1949 an assassin fired three bullets at Shah Mohammad Reza Pahlavi, ruler of Iran, from a distance of only six feet. All three bullets ripped through the Shah's hat and he escaped unharmed.

Cannonballs and artillery shells

The impacts of cannon balls and huge explosive shells have provided some unusual near misses. Smoothbore cannons, firing twelve-pound spherical shot, were widely used during the American Civil War. Col. Frank Haskell of the Union Army described some close brushes with cannon balls that he observed during the Battle of Gettysburg.

"Strange freaks these round shot play! We saw a man coming up from the rear with his full knapsack on, and some canteens of water held by straps in his hands. He was walking slowly and with apparent unconcern, though the iron hailed around him. A shot struck the knapsack, and it and its contents flew thirty yards in each direction, the knapsack disappearing like an egg thrown spitefully against a rock. The soldier stopped and turned about in puzzled surprise, put up one hand to his back to assure himself that the knapsack was not there, and then walked slowly on again unharmed, with not even his coat torn. Near us was a man crouching behind a small disintegrated stone, which was about the size of a common water bucket. He was bent up, with his face to the ground, in the attitude of a pagan worshipper before his idol. It looked so absurd to see him thus, that I went and said to him, 'Do not lie there like a toad. Why not go to your regiment and be a man?' He turned up his face, with a stupid, terrified look upon me, and then without a word turned his nose again to the ground. An orderly that was with me at the time told me a few moments later, that a shot struck the stone, smashing it in a thousand fragments, but did not touch the man, though his head was not six inches from the stone."

Explosive shells were also used in the Civil War. Lt. John C. Kinney of the Union Navy wrote of his near-death from such a shell while perched high on the mast of the USS *Hartford* during the Battle of Mobile Bay.

"The mast on which the writer [Kinney] was perched was twice struck, once slightly, and again just below the foretop, by a heavy shell from a rifle [rifled cannon] on the Confederate gunboat *Selma*. Fortunately the shell came tumbling end over end and buried itself in the mast, butt-end first, leaving the percussion-cap protruding. Had it come point first, or had it struck any other part of the mast than in the reinforced portion where the heel of the top mast laps the top of the lower mast, this contribution to the literature of war would probably have been lost to the world, as the distance to the deck was about a hundred feet. As it was, the sudden jar would have dislodged anyone from the crosstrees had not the shell been visible from the time it left the *Selma*, thus giving time to prepare for it by an extra grip around the top of the mast."

The expanding gases from an exploding shell create a blast wave which can, itself, kill. During World War I, hundreds of thousands of soldiers in the trenches were protected from shell fragments by crouching low, but they were still hit by the blast wave of a shell exploding in close proximity. One officer described the sensation as a great pressure against him which felt soft but was sufficiently powerful to knock him unconscious. Upon recovery such victims complained of headache, dizziness, lethargy, and inability to concentrate. They were said to be suffering from "shell shock."

Ernie Pyle, the American World War II war correspondent, interviewed Capt. Russell Wight, an infantry commander who on three occasions had German eighty-eight millimeter shells land within ten feet of him. In each case the exploding shells left him freakishly untouched, causing him no ill effects other than being deaf for about twenty-four hours after each concussion. He said that he had heard no explosions, and the only sensation was that of an enormous bear giving him a sudden hug.

Some victims have survived after being thrown large distances through the air by the blast wave of an exploding shell. Lt. Comdr. C. Trelawny, the captain of a British destroyer at World War I's Battle of Jutland, had a shell pass so close over him on the destroyer's bridge that it removed his cap and gave him a nasty scalp wound. All the others on the bridge, with the exception of two men, were killed when the shell exploded. The captain and the two others were blown twenty-four feet from the bridge into some wreckage. They extricated themselves and the captain brought the crippled ship safely back to port.

A shell exploding on the USS *San Francisco* during World War II hurled the ship's navigator, Comdr. Rae E. Arison, through the air. "It blew me clear across the bridge, passing between the wheel and the telegraph," Arison recalled. He hit the screen on the side of the bridge and passed out cold. After he regained consciousness, a second shell exploded below his position on the bridge.

"The force of the explosion blew me up and over," he recalled. "I made three complete turns in the air. Below me I could see the five-inch gun surrounded by a quarter-inch shield. If I hit the shield I would have been cut in two. My luck held and I landed feet first on the barrel of the gun. This fractured both legs. The gun was elevated about thirty degrees, so I slid down the barrel and landed in the gun captain's arms."

Bombs

Some survivors of bombings have also had notable escapes. Miles Mordaunt told of a strange bomb survival case that he witnessed one night during the London "blitz" of World War II.

"As we watched there was a shattering explosion in the

street, and the front of one house disappeared, leaving it like a series of superimposed stage sets, with the various rooms and their wallpapers all starkly shining in the red light [from fires]. At about the third floor one room stood out very sharply, for the white tiling—it was a bathroom —caught the light. We heard some wild calls, but it was impossible to tell where they were coming from at first. We walked toward the scene, and probably because the white tiling caught our eye, we looked up again, and could just make out a figure that seemed to be stuck to the wall. We found out afterward that a man was holding a towel rail in one hand, and standing precariously on a ridge consisting of about half a tile and the bit of cement holding it to the wall.

"Before we could get there the fire brigade was on the scene. The man was rescued and complained bitterly that he'd been left up there for days, as he thought, and had had a nightmare time screaming, when he thought nobody would come to his assistance." Actually the fire brigade had performed very efficiently.

Another interesting case was told by a former chief fire warden to Constantine Fitzgibbon, author of *The Blitz*.

"A pretty and extremely respectable girl was taking a bath when her parent's house was hit. By some fluke—and the effects of bomb blast were often extremely odd—the tub was tipped upside down, with the girl still in it, and thus provided her with shelter from the mass of bricks and rubble in which she was buried. The rescue men dug a shaft from the top to get the buried person out, and when they lifted the tub off her were not unnaturally surprised to discover a beautiful, naked, uninjured girl. Her reaction was one of acute embarrassment: East End girls are very modest. Warden Smith found a flannel nightdress in the rubble, filthy but still better than nothing, and this she gratefully put on at the bottom of the shaft. She was then hoisted up it by means of a block and tackle. Unfortunately on the way up her grimy nightdress caught on a nail or long splinter, and when she emerged at the top of the ruin she was once again as naked and pink as Venus rising from the

Cypriot sea. This time Warden Smith gave her his greatcoat. But so acute was her shame that, as he rather ruefully remarked, not only did she lack the courage to return him his overcoat, but to this day she always crosses to the far side of the Bow Road when she sees him coming toward her."

Another Londoner arrived home very late, not realizing that the house in which he lived had been sliced in two by a bomb. He went up the stairs and, fortunately for him, went to bed in the half-a-bedroom that still stood. Rescuers brought him down by ladder.

In 1944, a V-1 buzz bomb hit a house in which an elderly man was taking a bath. Nothing remained but debris, so there seemed little hope that the man could still be alive. However, rescuers dug down into the debris and found the man, dazed but unhurt, still sitting in the bathtub. Said he, "I don't know how it happened. I just pulled out the plug and the house blew up."

The atomic bombings in Japan also had their share of extraordinarily narrow escapes. Shigeyoshi Morimoto, whose home was in Nagasaki, had been working for months in Hiroshima, making antiaircraft kites for the Japanese Army. He was shopping for paintbrushes less than nine-hundred yards from ground zero when the first atomic bomb exploded. Morimoto was protected from the blast by the wreckage of the flimsy store and he then fled the city with three assistants, in a coal car, bound for Nagasaki and safety.

After reaching his home in Nagasaki, Morimoto was breathlessly telling his wife about the terrible bomb that had been dropped on Hiroshima when there was a blinding blue flash. He flung back a trap door in the floor and shoved his wife and infant son into the shelter. Morimoto was to survive two atomic bombings.

Morimoto was not the only person to survive both atomic bombings. Nine employees of the Mitsubishi Shipbuilding Company had been sent from its Nagasaki plant to work temporarily at its Hiroshima shipyards. All nine survived the Hiroshima bomb, returned to Nagasaki, and survived the second bomb there.

A Buddhist priest was praying in a temple at Hiroshima when the bomb exploded. The enormous pillars holding up the temple collapsed and the ceiling fell down toward him. However, there was an opening just above him—created where the bomb had blasted away a roof tile—and the hole saved him as the heavy roof crashed all around him. He simply pulled himself up through the opening and was saved.

Adventures inside a bomb blast

Ernie Pyle gave one of the most graphic accounts of what it was like to survive a nearby non-nuclear bomb blast in his book *Brave Men.*

"We correspondents stayed in a villa run by the Fifth Army's Public Relations Section. In that house lived five officers, twelve enlisted men, and a dozen correspondents, both American and British.

"The villa was located on the waterfront. The current sometimes washed over our back steps. The house was a huge, rambling affair with four stories down on the beach and then another complete section of three stories just above it on the bluff, all connected by a series of interior stairways.

"For weeks long-range artillery shells had been hitting in the water or on shore within a couple hundred yards of us. Raiders came over nightly, yet ever since D-day the villa had seemed to be charmed.

"Most of the correspondents and staff lived in the part of the house down by the water, it being considered the safer because it was lower down. But I had been sleeping alone in a room in the top part because it was a lighter place to work in the daytime. We called it 'Shell Alley' up there because the Anzio-bound shells seemed to come in a groove right past our eaves day and night.

"One night Sergeant Slim Aarons of *Yank* magazine said, 'Those shells are so close that if the German gunner had just hiccuped when he fired, bang would have gone our house.' And I said, 'It seems to me we've about used up our luck. It's inevitable that this house will be hit before we leave here.'

"The very next morning I awakened early and was just lying there for a few minutes before getting up. It was only seven o'clock but the sun was out bright.

"Suddenly the antiaircraft guns let loose. Ordinarily I didn't get out of bed during a raid, but I did get up that time. I was sleeping in long underwear and a shirt, so I just put on my steel helmet, slipped on some wool-lined slippers, and went to the window for a look at the shooting.

"I had just reached the window when a terrible blast swirled me around and threw me into the middle of the room. I don't remember whether I heard any noise or not. The half of the window that was shut was ripped out and hurled across the room. The glass was blown into thousands of little pieces. Why the splinters or the window frame itself didn't hit me, I don't know.

"From the moment of the first blast until it was over probably not more than fifteen seconds passed. Those fifteen seconds were so fast and confusing that I truly can't say what took place. The other correspondents reported the same.

"There was debris flying back and forth all over the room. One gigantic explosion came after another. The concussion was terrific. It was like a great blast of air in which my body felt as light and as helpless as a leaf tossed in a whirlwind. I jumped into one corner of the room and squatted down and just cowered there. I definitely thought it was the end. Outside of that I don't remember what my emotions were.

"Suddenly one whole wall of my room flew in, burying the bed—where I'd been a few seconds before—under hundreds of pounds of brick, stone, and mortar. Later when we dug out my sleeping bag we found the steel frame of the bed broken and twisted. If I hadn't gone to the window I would have had at least two broken legs and a crushed chest.

"Then the wooden doors were ripped off their hinges

and crashed into the room. Another wall started to tumble, but caught partway down. The French doors leading to the balcony blew out and one of my chairs was upended through the open door.

"As I sat cowering in the corner, I remember fretting because my steel hat had blown off with the first blast and I couldn't find it. Later I found it right beside me.

"I was astonished at feeling no pain, for debris went tearing around every inch of the room and I couldn't believe I hadn't been hit. But the only wound I got was a tiny cut on my right cheek, from flying glass, and I didn't even know when that happened. The first I knew of it was when blood ran down my chin and dropped onto my hand.

"I had several unfinished dispatches lying on my table, and the continuing blasts scattered them helter-skelter over the room and holes were punched in the paper. I remember thinking, 'Well, it won't make any difference now anyhow.'

"Finally the terrible nearby explosions ceased and gradually the ack-ack died down and at last I began to have some feeling of relief that it was over and I was still alive. But I stayed crouched in the corner until the last shot was fired.

"When the bombing was all over, my room was a shambles, the sort of thing you see only in the movies. More than half the room was knee-deep with broken brick and tiles and mortar. The other half was a disarray covered with plaster dust and broken glass. My typewriter was full of mortar and broken glass, but was not damaged.

"My pants had been lying on the chair that went through the door, so I dug them out from under the debris, put them on, and started down to the other half of the house.

"Down below everything was a mess. The ceilings had come down upon men still in bed. Some beds were a foot deep in debris. That nobody was killed was a pure miracle.

"Bill Strand of the Chicago *Tribune* was out in the littered hallway in his underwear, holding his left arm. Major Jay Vessels of Duluth, Minnesota, was running around without a stitch of clothing. We checked rapidly and found that everybody was still alive.

"The boys couldn't believe it when they saw me coming in. Wick Fowler had thought the bombs had made direct hits on the upper part of the house. He had just said to George Tucker of the Associated Press, 'Well, they got Ernie.'

"But after they saw I was all right they began to laugh and called me 'Old Indestructible.' I guess I was the luckiest man in the house, at that, although Old Dame Fortune was certainly riding with all of us that morning.

"The German raiders had dropped a whole stick of bombs right across our area. They were apparently five-hundred pounders, and they hit within thirty feet of our house.

"Many odd things happened, as they do in all bombings. Truthfully, I don't remember my walls coming down at all, though I must have been looking at them when they fell. Oddly, the wall that fell on my bed was across the room from where the bomb hit. In other words, it fell toward the bomb. That was caused by the bomb's terrific blast creating a vacuum; when air rushed back to the center of that vacuum, its power was as great as the original rush of air outward.

"When I went to put on my boots there was broken glass clear into the toes of them. My mackinaw had been lying on the foot of the bed and was covered with hundreds of pounds of debris, yet my goggles in the pocket were unbroken.

"At night I always put a pack of cigarettes on the floor beside my bed. When I went to get a cigarette, I found they'd all been blown out of the pack.

"The cot occupied by Bob Vermillion of the United Press was covered a foot deep with broken tile and plaster. When it was all over somebody heard him call out plaintively, 'Will somebody come and take this stuff off of me?'

"After seeing the other correspondents, I went back to my shattered room to look around again, and in came Sgt. Bob Geake of Fort Wayne, Indiana, the first sergeant of our outfit. He had some iodine and was going around painting up those who had been scratched. Bob took out a dirty handkerchief, spit on it two or three times, then washed the blood off my face before putting on the iodine. You could hardly call that the last word in sterilization.

"Three of the other boys were rushed off to the tent hospital. After an hour or so, five of us drove out in a jeep to see how they were. They were not in bad shape, and we sat around a stove in one of the tents and drank coffee and talked with some of the officers.

"By then my head and ears had started to ache from the concussion blasts, and several of the others were feeling the same, so the doctors gave us codeine and aspirin.

"Much to my surprise, I wasn't weak or shaky after it was all over. In fact I felt fine—partly buoyed up by elation over still being alive, I suppose. But by noon I began to get jumpy, and by midafternoon I felt very old and 'beat up,' as they say, and the passage of the afternoon shells over our house really gave me the willies.

"We got Italian workmen in to clean up the debris, and by evening all the rooms had been cleared, shaky walls knocked down, and blankets hung at the window for blackout.

"All except my room. It was so bad they decided it wasn't worth cleaning up, so we dug out my sleeping bag, gathered up my scattered stuff, and I shifted to another room. But then the hospital invited Wick Fowler and me to move out with them, saying they'd put up a tent for us. We took them up on it. We thought there was such a thing as pressing our luck too far in one spot.

"In the next few days little memories of the bombing gradually came back into my consciousness. I remembered I had smoked a whole pack of cigarettes that morning. And I recalled how I went to take my pocket comb out of my shirt pocket, to comb my hair, but instead actually took my handkerchief out of my hip pocket and started combing my hair with the handkerchief.

"Me nervous? I should say not."

Lethal missiles of nature

Not all lethal projectiles are man-made as are bullets, artillery shells, and bombs. Some are formed by nature. For example, in Chapter Fourteen we saw that Haroun Tazieff suffered a grazing blow from a falling, molten volcanic bomb. Another very dangerous missile of nature is the unusually large hailstone. Violent hailstorms with oversized hail have caused some terrible massacres of victims caught in the open. In 1932 a Chinese hailstorm killed two hundred people in western Hunan Province and injured thousands. In 1888 history's worst recorded hailstorm killed 246 people in the northern Indian city of Moradabad. The hailstones, which were as large as cricket balls, reportedly killed everyone unlucky enough to be caught in the open. A hailstorm in the Jablah coastal area of Syria destroyed the crops of forty out of fifty-three villages in 1978, threatening sixty-thousand people with starvation.

In August 1857 some fishermen in an open boat found themselves in great peril when a violent hailstorm began to pelt Messina, Italy. The hailstones smashed roofs and vegetation, injured many people scurrying for cover, and killed a child. The fishermen, in danger of being beaten to death by the hailstones, saved themselves by jumping into the water and sheltering themselves under their boat.

Another of nature's deadly projectiles is the meteorite. Has anyone ever been killed by a meteorite impact? There is no well-authenticated case of any meteorite-caused death, although there is one known case in which a meteorite struck an Alabama woman a glancing blow in 1954, bruising her thigh. There have been a few other near misses. In 1982 a six-pound meteorite crashed through the roof of a home in Wethersfield, Connecticut, and landed in the living room where Robert and Wanda Donahue were watching television. Neither was injured. A decade earlier, another meteorite had crashed into another Wethersfield house a mile away.

A runaway buzz saw blade

Many man-made objects, not intended to be violent projectiles, have become such as a result of accidents. In one case a buzz saw blade tore loose in a Florida sawmill, ripped through the side of the mill, and then cut its way through the side of a nearby house. The whirling blade sliced a kitchen table neatly in two as the astonished resident was eating breakfast, and continued on its way out the other side of the house.

ABOUT THE AUTHOR

JOHN ADAMS is an author/soil scientist/orange grower.
He has a Ph.D in soil science and worked for seven years
as a U.S. Government soil scientist. His first book, *Dirt*, is
a popular science book about soil, and he is currently
working on a book entitled *The Disappearing Orange*,
which will focus on Southern California in the days when
it was filled with citrus groves. He is owner of the last
orange grove in a Southern California town which was
formerly a community based almost entirely on orange
growing.